Excerpts from

[handwritten: 12-20-09   Dear Michaela, Because I Know my mom would ... you ... y! ... , Christine]

S0-BAW-996

Voices from a Vanished Past

Memories of a Christian Childhood in Hitler's Germany

Simone Feldman

WISDOM FOUNDATION PUBLISHING
Honolulu, Hawai'i

EXCERPTS FROM VOICES FROM A VANISHED
PAST: MEMORIES OF A CHRISTIAN CHILDHOOD
IN HITLER'S GERMANY

Copyright © 2006
Wisdom Factors International
All rights reserved.

ISBN 932590-04-1-6

Published by

Wisdom Foundation Publishing
PO Box 61599
Honolulu, Hawaii 96839
USA

Phone: 808-988-4191
Fax: 808-988-4212
www.wisdomfactors.com
info@wisdomfactors.com

Please contact the publisher for organization bulk orders of
Excerpts from Voices from a Vanished Past

1 2 3 4 5 6 7 8 9 10

Excerpts from

VOICES FROM A VANISHED PAST

Memories of a Christian Childhood in Hitler's Germany

TABLE OF CONTENTS

To forget one's ancestors
is to be
a brook without a source,
a tree without a root.
(Chinese proverb)

This book is dedicated to my parents,
Johannes and Gertrud Zimmermann,
and to all the innocent victims of
violence and war.

Foreword

When my wife, Simone Feldman, was diagnosed on June 22, 2006, with cancer of the pancreas, we both knew I would not be able to complete the editing of the English version of *Voices from a Vanished Past* in time for her to see the entire book. Consequently, she asked that we take the chapters already edited—a little more than half the complete text—and print them for family and friends. Her request was straightforward. "I want to be able to hold a book in my hands before I go."

With encouragement from M. Jan Rumi, president of Wisdom Factors International, and technical assistance from Bishop Stephen Randolph Sykes, our man for all seasons, we have been able to put together the volume you are about to read. Actually, it includes the primary chapters and is in fact what Simone and I put together for our literary agent to present to possible commercial publishers. That process is going forward as I write these lines in early August. We hope it will be successful before too long.

Meantime, I hope you enjoy the 200-odd pages that await you. Although I am a biased reader, I find this book a fascinating testimony to the courage of a little girl caught up in one of the most toxic social environments of modern times. The Nazi scourge of Jews, socialists, homosexuals, Romany people, and the handicapped is well-known. Less so is the poisonous impact on ordinary German families like the Zimmermanns and their friends.

As Simone prepares to leave this world, I see the same courage in her now at 75 and am honored to have had the chance to collaborate with her on this extraordinary manifestation of personal wisdom. May it and the full version that follows bring us greater understanding of the darkness and redemptive light of human experience and above all help a little to move this world closer to the peace that passes all understanding: Shalom, salaam, Friede.

Reynold Feldman
Honolulu
August 2006

Preface

I often ask myself why I have retained such clear memories, reaching back in many instances to my earliest childhood. This questionable gift has astounded not only family members but friends and acquaintances as well. Does it have a purpose? It should, because I have come to believe that nothing happens in life without a purpose.

As I write these words, I am 68 years old and have traveled a long road from the remotest corner of northeastern Europe, East Prussia (now Poland and Russia), to the southwestern-most part of the United States, the Hawaiian Islands. This journey has taken me through different villages, cities, and countries, with resting places along the way where I collected new experiences. These stops—and experiences—happened not always by choice but were often caused by circumstances beyond my or my family's control. What we call history had a big impact on the development of my emotional, physical, and spiritual life.

The Bible teaches that God works in history to punish, reward, and restore his people. This large-scale action may also apply to individual lives. There is another element in the realm of the Divine, however, that is mysterious, that may change certain events and situations in an instant. We call it Grace. Often we forget that God's guidance and love have been present from the beginning of our lives. But we humans, either through arrogance or bitterness, have closed our eyes and ears to this reality.

Like so many of my fellow travelers on this planet, I came to points in my life when I asked the big questions:

Why am I here? What is this all about? What is my purpose? Is my journey pre-destined, or is it simply the result of the never-ceasing interplay of natural forces? I was about six years old when I experienced a moment like this for the first time. I was playing in my grandmother's backyard. Suddenly I stopped playing in the sand, looked at my hands and feet, and something in me asked: "What are you doing? Why are you here?" It was a sobering second of consciousness. In that instant I no longer felt like a child. I felt ageless. An instant later I returned to my play.

Now, so many years later, I am sometimes struck with awe when I look back at all the turmoil in my past and consider that today I am living with a loving family in a free country and, thanks to an awareness of a Higher Power guiding me, have peace of mind. Since there may not be too many miles of the journey left, I feel an inner urge to translate these memories into words—memories which run through my mind like a movie, replete with soundtrack and pictures. I am writing this book not only for my grown children but more especially for my future grandchildren who may ask questions about their German granny who lived as a child in Germany during those darkest years of the Twentieth Century. Being one of the few remaining members of my generation that remember specific events from the daily life of those times, I now understand that my vivid memories were stored in my mind for this purpose. They tell about the life my family, our neighbors, and I lived. Nothing more and nothing less. They do not excuse or exonerate any of the terrible things done by individual German men and women. Like it or not, the powerful dark forces which paralyzed so many souls in my nation have cast a permanent shadow over the history of my country.

Years ago, when I was a young immigrant, someone

asked me sarcastically, "Where were you when they hunted down all the Jews in your country?" Shocked, I answered, "I did not witness anything like that. I went to school every day like all the other children my age around the world." "Yes," he replied, "and your farmers fed their pigs too!" This person was neither Jewish nor European but had grown up in a New York City filled with a self-justified gospel of hate. No German-Jewish survivor of the Camps I met over the years has ever addressed me like that man. They knew from experience about the plight of so many Germans of their generation—victims in their own way of the Nazi curse.

Now that this book will be shared beyond the confines of my family, I hope what you read will add to your understanding of the human tragedy and Divine comedy that people from the beginning of the world have experienced and that my memories will cause you to reflect on your own life and the lessons it has provided you with thus far.

Finally, should anything written here hurt someone's feelings, I ask for forgiveness in advance.

Simone Feldman
Kane'ohe, O'ahu
22 July 1999

❖

1

Mutti 's Voice, 1990

Saint Paul, Minnesota

I still feel her spirit around me and hear her voice in my head. Most of her belongings, like her little white desk, are just as they were in her room. She left the desk neatly organized before she went to the hospital for the last time. It still brings tears to my eyes when I look at it, and I am not ready to change anything yet.

I see her sitting in her armchair next to the window, her embroidery implements near her on the small table. Despite her disability, she had picked up embroidery again, a craft she had enjoyed in her younger years. With iron discipline and help from a wooden frame, she had managed to do this work with her one good hand. (The left side of her body had been partially paralyzed by a stroke in 1972.) She had even taught herself to thread a needle without any help from others.

So, embroidery had become her daily work for some years, punctuated by long hours of reading while she rested in her bed in the afternoon. She wanted to make up for the years lost when she was too busy with her family and household chores to read. Now she had the opportunity to go through all the books that had been forbidden during the Third Reich. She was also a poet, writing brief lyrics for the birthdays of relatives and friends. Not least, her

1

room served as a place of refuge for all the family members, including Winston, the big, black cat—and me.

While concentrating on her handwork, she would often tell stories from her past. In this way, I got information about my parents' whereabouts and activities during the years before my birth. I could never get enough of it. These intimate moments with Mutti were among her greatest gifts to me.

Speak to me now, Mutti. I am tuned in!

Your father and I knew each other from the time we played together in the sandbox. Our parents were friends. Both our fathers worked for the *deutsche Reichsbahn* [German Imperial Railway] in the City of Allenstein, where we grew up.

As a young man, Grandpa Karl Zimmermann, your father's father, and Grandpa Ernst Radtke on my side had been trained as locomotive engineers. They initially drove trains originating in Osterode, a smaller town south of Allenstein, where they met their future wives—Dorothea-Marie Nickel and Lina Arndt, respectively. Dashing young men, they were considered "captains of the rails," with a status similar back then, in the late 1800s, to that of airline pilots in the 1950s. It was the dream of many boys in those days to become railroad engineers when they grew up.

Now here's something I've never told you. Oma [Grandma] Marie—she was always called by her second name—had been promised in marriage by her parents to a wealthy farmer in the area, a widower. She was so smitten by Opa [Grandpa] Karl, however, that she eloped with him and lived with his mother until they could get married.

Well, getting back to my story, I was born in Osterode in 1905. In 1914, when World War I broke out,

I was eight, just the same age as you when the Second World War began. Isn't that strange? We fled before the approaching Russian Army. After Field Marshall von Hindenburg won the Battle of Tannenberg, we were able to return home. But the Russians were the victors the second time around, and our families lost everything. We were lucky to escape with our lives, as you know from your own experience.

Your father was too young to be drafted to fight in World War I. He had been born in Allenstein in 1901, so he was only thirteen when the War began. Seventeen when it ended, he along with his classmates was sent to one of the large farms in the region to help with the harvest. The food shortage back then was even worse than after World War II. Everyone was on a near-starvation diet. Look at that photo of Pappa from those days, the one where he is wearing a bathing suit. You can count every rib!

Opa Ernst, my father, drove trains back and forth between Allenstein and the front. As a result, he never became a soldier. Still, that didn't mean he was out of harm's way. One day after returning home, he showed us his hat. There was a fresh bullet hole right through it. An inch or two lower, and that would have been that. What had seemed to be a stray horse galloping alongside the train turned out to be a Russian mare with a Cossack hanging onto the side and shooting at Opa from underneath the horse's belly. The intention had been to stop the train. Thank God the shooter failed. The thought of how close Opa had come to death sent chills running down my back. Mother was crying and hugging him. Hanna, my older sister, was leaning against a door. She had gone white as a sheet.

After the Kaiser fled to Holland in 1918, the

fighting finally stopped. The whole country was left in a state of utter chaos. There was famine throughout the land. Former soldiers in tattered uniforms went around begging in the streets alongside homeless families. Many died of exhaustion. You were lucky if you had some friends who were farmers. We would take tree bark, grind and mix it with a little flour, and make bread. The fighting had ceased because the nations involved were exhausted, but what followed was not what we had hoped.

The Treaty of Versailles did not really bring peace. An underground restlessness remained which led to extreme nationalism and social unrest in both Germany and the other European nations. The Weimar Republic, established as a democracy in 1919, was unable to cope and failed for this reason. The French and Italian soldiers occupying our town added insult to injury. They routinely kicked pedestrians off the sidewalk when they felt the latter were in the way and abused them verbally with terms like "German dogs." The common person felt betrayed and deprived not only of physical and spiritual nourishment but of human dignity as well.

Gradually, rumors about treachery on the former home front began to circulate. The phrase "stab in the back," alluding to the betrayal-murder of the hero Siegfried in the Nordic legend, was soon heard everywhere. Later on, Dr. Goebbels' Nazi propaganda machine made good use of this slogan by telling the crowds that the misery of the German people following the lost World War and even the defeat itself had been caused by the treachery of German Jews, who through their self-serving habits and culture had sold the country out.

You may ask why intelligent people could believe nonsense like this. Well, there were many opportunists who bought into the Nazi ideology early on, while others adopted it wholeheartedly like a new religion. The uneducated masses did not know any better. Generation after generation they had been trained to be obedient subjects of their kings. They did not question authority. They simply wanted work, bread, and a strong fatherland of which they could once again be proud. Democracy for them was just a word, a foreign concept that meant nothing. To blame the ruling houses of Europe for their dilemma would never have crossed their minds. No, the smallest group among us became a scapegoat and was blamed for everything.

You ask where we were, Father and I, during this period. Father had finished high school by 1919 and was enrolled in a teacher-training college in my home town, Osterode. I was still attending middle school, which I finished in 1921. But in 1920 a terrible Asian flu hit Germany's undernourished population, and people died like flies. My older sister was struck too. Although she finally recovered, she was never the same after that. The ferocious fever had taken its toll on her delicate constitution. The most artistic in our family, she played piano, painted, and—when she was well—did intricate embroidery. She never married, though, and at the end of World War II she died a horrible death.

I was the family tomboy. I liked sports, played tennis, and most of all I enjoyed riding—something I was able to do whenever I visited my relatives in the country.

I was not afraid of anything, even when I was very small. An incident comes to mind. I was about seven. We had just moved from Osterode to Allenstein when a visit by the Crown Prince and Princess was announced to the public. Mother, Hanna, and I joined the crowd lining the Kaiser-Wilhelm Allee to greet the royal couple with little flags and flowers. As the fancy open carriage finally moved toward us, I broke free of the crowd, raced into the street, and jumped onto the lowest step, at the same time flinging a bouquet of flowers onto the lovely princess's lap. She spontaneously held my arms and gazed at me with a warm, surprised smile until two policemen took me away. I didn't even care when Mother scolded me. I had looked into the beautiful blue-green eyes of a real princess. Nobody could take that away from me.

Pappa's college classrooms had been turned into hospital wards during the flu epidemic, since everyone had come down with the bug, including him. A faded snapshot in our surviving family album shows him during those times. The food in the refectory was so horrible, he said, it was a wonder any of us recovered. One evening a classmate of his was sent to his room for offering the following table grace: "For the swill before us, I offer You my grateful grunts!" *["Fuer diesen schlunz, ich Dir gruentz'!"]* He then flung his still-full plate into the dumb waiter and sent it to the kitchen.

To be sure, the year 1920 contained a happy event for us as well. The Allied Powers allowed our province of East Prussia to hold a *Volksabstimmung*, or plebiscite. This meant the citizens could decide for themselves whether our province should belong to the German Reich or Poland. The result was overwhelmingly pro-Germany (99%). As a result, the government declared a provincial day of rejoicing—*Deutscher Tag*, or German Day, as it was called. We schoolgirls, asked to help as volunteers with the preparation, were overjoyed. However, our happiness did not diminish the fact that East Prussia remained physically cut off from the main body of the German Reich by the so-called Polish Corridor.

Hans received his teaching degree in 1922 as valedictorian [*primus*] of his class. He even sent me a beautiful invitation card meant for "special guests" to the commencement ceremony. His outstanding achievement notwithstanding, the state was short of funds, and there were no teaching positions in sight. Fortunately, he played the piano very well. In fact, he and some musically inclined friends had created a music club call "Arion" during their last year of high school. Returning to his hometown, he re-established the old group, gave piano lessons, and for a while became a mathematics tutor. One day he and another member of Arion were hired to play background music for the silent pictures at the new movie house in town. For some reason, everyone called the theater the *Floh-Kino*, or flea cinema. One can only guess why! Jobs being scare, they accepted right away. Everybody back then needed whatever income they could scratch together.

In winter, the heating system at the theater worked only sporadically and then not very well. So, to keep themselves warm and their fingers limber, Hans and his friend resorted to a mixture of hot tea and rum. In some of the early German films, directors tried to dramatize social injustices with a split-screen technique. In the top part you would see elegant people enjoying a fancy-dress ball while below, poor folks shared a dark, dank cellar with rats and roaches. Consequently, the mood of the music had to change back and forth quickly—no easy job for our freezing virtuosos!

On one particular below-zero New Year's Eve— Hans told this story often, always to our amusement—he and his partner had taken on a little too much anti-freeze. As a result, they missed a rather important scene and mood change. Instead of playing Chopin's familiar funeral march to accompany a rather solemn scene, they were still clinking away with the perky strains of "The March of the Dwarves on Watch" ["*Heinzelmaennchens Wachtparade*"]

7

from the preceding sequence. The sight of the somber pallbearers quick-stepping their way to these joyful strains was too much for the audience. It was only when the house broke into peals of laughter that our now-warm pianists realized their mistake.

We saw each other as often as possible. On Sundays our families got together for long walks through the beautiful forests which surrounded our town. Cakes had been baked at home and packed in baskets. After walking for two hours, we would arrive at a forest restaurant, with a prominent sign in front: "Families can brew their own coffee here." For that privilege, the proprietor took only a small fee. Slowly, some pleasures were returning to daily life.

In 1923 we were engaged, but marriage had to wait until Hans could find a secure position as a teacher. Meanwhile, I took a bookkeeping job in the neighborhood and tried to save enough money for my dowry. Then, just as your father had accepted a job in a bank, inflation suddenly swept through the land. Hans was now dealing with millions and billions of paper Reich-Marks. The prices fluctuated from day to day. Mostly, they went up. Once again, hungry, desperate people were roaming the streets. A loaf of bread that cost 1 million Marks one day might cost 2 million the next. Examples of this nearly worthless paper money are pasted in our old photo album. There you will also see snapshots of Hans's mother, Oma Dorchen, who lost the balance of her inheritance to the inflation. As a result, Pappa's dream of doing advanced studies in mathematics at the University of Koenigsberg evaporated. His younger brother, Erich, was still in high school, so the remaining funds had to be used for him.

At last in January 1925, Pappa got a job as a mathematics teacher at the military academy in Allenstein, a garrison town. With our future looking a little more secure, we got married in March. The wedding took place in the town of Neidenburg, where your Grandpa Ernst's parents lived. They were celebrating their golden anniversary the same day, so we had a kind of joint party. We also took a picture together, but none of us looks happy in it. The studio was freezing cold, and the photographer was drunk. It is the worst wedding picture I've ever seen.

We rented a small apartment in my parents' neighborhood, and your sister Gerda was born in December. When she was two, your father accepted a short-term teaching job at a Protestant school in the mainly Catholic town of Roessel. The town was dominated by an ancient Crusader castle that had been restored and was in good condition. After the spring-summer term, he got the position of principal at a country school in the nearby village of Worplack. Thank God, we were finally able to settle down!

In the autumn of 1927 we moved into a beautiful brick school house with long windows and a high ceiling. It had two wings, one with classrooms and the other, our living quarters. In the front there was the large schoolyard. In the back, a private garden bordered on a round pond. Then there were the mighty linden trees scenting the air in spring with the fragrance of their little blossoms and providing cool shade on the hot summer days. *Ach ja,* looking back, I realize that these were the happiest years of my life. We were young, full of hope, and the world seemed poised before us with untold new experiences.

Of course, I had a lot to learn. Life in the country was not easy at first for a city girl like me. As cozy as the house was, it lacked all the modern conveniences like toilets, running water, even electricity. Can you imagine? If you wanted to wash clothes, clean the dishes, or take a bath, you had to pump water outside, carry it in by the bucket, and heat it on the large, coal- or wood-fed brick oven in the kitchen. The outhouses were located at the rear of the schoolyard, illuminated at night by oil lamps. After a few weeks, I was exhausted. Pappa knew I needed some help with the heavy household chores, so he hired Martha, a local peasant girl, to assist me during the day.

As a boy Pappa had spent many a summer with his mother's relatives in the country. As a result, he had learned how to work the soil and to garden. Soon we were having a lot of fun planting all kinds of vegetables and flowers together. From a book we learned how to preserve what we harvested, including juices we made, in glass containers and store them for use during the long East Prussian winters. Although teaching was considered an honorable profession, the salaries in those days were meager, so all this helped us get by.

The soil was rich, and everything grew in abundance. At the end of summer we had loads of cucumbers and pumpkins, which we pickled and stored in large jars. They lasted the whole year. Our garden also contained wonderful cherry, plum, apple, and pear trees. We preserved large quantities, gave a lot away to the school children, and sold the rest at the market in the nearest town, which yielded a little extra pocket money for me.

Meantime, some of the local farm women taught me the fine art of raising poultry—chicken, ducks, geese, and turkeys. As fate would have it, there was an unused barn next to the schoolyard which was the perfect place for our livestock. Once a turkey hen went missing for a number of days. I thought a fox must surely have gotten her. I had nearly forgotten about the hen when one day she showed up in our garden with twelve little turkey chicks. She must have sensed I was a novice in country matters and went off to build a secret nest somewhere in the bushes. From this experience I concluded that the demeaning expression *dumme Pute* ("stupid turkey") in our language was totally inappropriate.

In the beginning of my poultry-raising career, I also managed to get the eggs mixed up. Fortunately, the animals were able to sort through my confusion. One day, clucking proudly, the fluffy yellow Leghorn hen strode into the yard with five ducklings and five chicks in tow. This foster arrangement worked fine at first, the hen was a good mom. But you should have seen the spectacle when one morning the ducklings took off for the pond, leaving a panic-stricken mother hen pacing up and down the bank, her wings flapping wildly. Yes, working with animals proved both rewarding and lots of fun.

For us, the bad years as far as food was concerned had ended. The majority of the population, however, still lived in poverty. The job market was at its lowest point. Craftsmen could not afford to take on apprentices, because the orders received were too few, and not many parents had the funds to give their children a post-school education. Only a small elite group could afford it.

Beggars and gypsies roamed the countryside. Each evening we had to make sure all the doors and windows were locked. For our safety, we also got ourselves a black boxer we named Rigo. One night when your father had to stay in Roessel for a meeting, Rigo protected me from great danger. Gerda was already in bed, and I was folding

11

laundry when I heard a knock at the door. Rigo, who was lying next to me, jumped up and, growling and giving out low, menacing barks, ran to the door. I asked who was there. A husky man's voice replied that he had met my husband in town and that the latter had given him a package to deliver. He apologized for coming so late. As I was about to turn the key and open the door, Rigo with a furious bark jumped against the door and knocked the key out of my hand. Then I knew something was very wrong, so I told the man to come back the next day, when I knew Hans would be home. Murmuring "good night," he walked away. I ran to the window in the next room. Through it in the moonlight I could see a tall figure with a broad-brimmed hat moving down the street.

The next day I read in the local newspaper that the police were searching for a dangerous criminal who had escaped from the local jail a few days before. I was sure that that was my "delivery man," especially when Pappa told me he had never given anyone a parcel to take to me. Good old Rigo!

Pappa's job in the beginning was quite challenging. Half his pupils were children of farmhands from the nearby *Rittergut* (baronial estate). Whenever the season required it, they were kept at home to help out. As a result, they missed a lot of school, and their academic achievements were slight to nonexistent. Then there was the matter of personal hygiene, or lack of it. When the weather permitted, Pappa kept the windows open wide.

He was shocked to learn that some of their older siblings were still illiterate even after leaving elementary school. An example was our maid, Martha. She could not even count to ten. Sometimes that got on my nerves. But considering her background, I could only feel pity for her and made repeated attempts to teach her to do basic household tasks. The farm workers' quarters were overcrowded. In some cases up to four children had to sleep in one bed. No wonder they were tired and inattentive in class. Poor Martha! I guess she was doing the best she could.

It did not take Pappa long to start working to change the centuries-old feudal arrangements on the estate. It was of course convenient for the landlords to have farm hands with strong backs and weak minds working for them for next to nothing. After all, what else could these poor creatures do? They really had no choice. As a convinced social democrat, Pappa believed that everyone should have a fair chance in life. This belief was strengthened by his Christian upbringing. So one day he paid a visit to Herr von Frankenfeld, the land owner. After a stormy debate, the latter took Pappa on a tour of the estate, including the workers' quarters. By his own admission, the Baron had not done this himself for years—leaving issues of worker management to his trusted estate supervisor, who always gave satisfactory reports.

As the two men rode toward the workers' quarters in Herr von Frankenfeld's one-horse gig, Pappa pointed to the miserable huts and said, "Your horse barns and pig sties are in far better shape than these hovels, Herr Baron! Will the children who live in such circumstances ever develop into healthy, productive members of your future work force? The classroom alone can never overcome such handicaps."

The Baron was at first speechless, then muttered some excuses like, "I had no idea. No one ever told me. I will speak with my supervisor as soon as possible." At this point, he stopped the gig in order to visit one of the huts. The family members who had thus far seen their master only fleetingly from a distance were shocked. But Herr von Frankenfeld seemed shocked too as he began to realize how broad the gap was between his privileged life and the living conditions of his workers.

"Herr Zimmermann," the Baron finally said. "I had no idea how rundown everything here has become. I shall talk with my supervisor immediately."

Such neglect of one's fellow human beings was always incomprehensible for your father. An educated Christian gentleman should know better, he thought. Even many years later when he would tell this story, his forehead would break into lines of concern. He would add that in those days even the big estates were struggling with inflation and the other ravages that succeeded the Great War. Still, the owners always managed to live well. There was simply no excuse, he felt, for the degrading conditions under which their hard-working peasant families were forced to live.

As it happened, Pappa's visit had had its effect. After the harvest that year, the Baron ordered many of the peasants' living quarters repaired and enlarged. Above all, stricter guidelines were established for regular school attendance. For my part, I taught the older girls how to sew simple things, to repair torn clothing, and to darn socks. I also showed them the rudiments of knitting and needlepoint. Among them I found some real talents.

In the country it was common knowledge that you could make soap from animal bones. So, the obvious lack of personal hygiene was not the result of a shortage of soap. I encouraged the girls not only to make more soap but to make more use of it. As a result, they began washing themselves, their hair, and their clothes more frequently. I told them that lack of money did not require a person to neglect her personal appearance. They agreed, and their new practice soon boosted their self-confidence. Some

mothers, saying they had their hands full with work and raising their boys, thanked me for my efforts.

Unfortunately, one also found children that had been physically abused by their alcoholic fathers. These boys and girls were not only undernourished but so dazed and closed up from this unnatural treatment by a parent that they could barely function in the classroom. Only later in the 30's did these families get helped through the *Mutterhilfsdienst* [Help for Mothers Program] established by the National Socialist Party. This was one of the positive initiatives taken in their early days by the Nazis. Another was the *Arbeitsdienstlager* [Work-Service Camps] established in the countryside for the jobless, hungry youth roaming the streets in the bigger cities. There were several such camps in East Prussia. Their goal was to clear the vast swamps in the lake district called Masuren [Masovia] , where the very first known inhabitants of the land, the Masovkens, had lived together with a Baltic tribe, the Pruskens, from whom the name *Preussen* [Prussia] derives.

This sort of project, to reclaim and cultivate swampland, had already been undertaken in the 12th and 13th Centuries by German Knights of the Cross, on their way to the Crusades in the Holy Land. These very same knights had caused the mighty brick fortresses of East Prussia to be built, around which the Province's walled cities grew up. Centuries later, the Polish King would offer German farmers land in his nearby kingdom as an incentive for them to settle in Poland and reclaim swampy land there.

Of course, under the then-new Hitler regime, this reclamation work in Germany was done beneath the banner of *Volksgemeinschaft* [the people' community]. In exchange for their work, the impoverished young men were given nutritious food, clean if simple shelter, good air, and a program of organized sports. Many of them felt that the neat, new uniforms had helped restore their sense of manly pride. For them, Hitler seemed a savior. Little did they realize that like the legendary Pied Piper of Hamlin (with whom der Fuehrer was occasionally compared after the War), Hitler was preparing them and others like them all over the country to become cannon fodder in his bid to conquer Europe.

We are having another beautiful summer evening in Saint Paul. I lean back in Mutti's comfortable armchair next to the window. A soft breeze makes the branches of the old trees dance against the orange sky. My eyes follow the wings of a bird as it disappears into the golden glow. The thought occurs to me: This day will soon count as tomorrow's past.

I remember more of what Mutti had told me about her life in what would become her favorite place in the East Prussian *Heimat* [homeland].

Through my love of horses and riding, I became friends with the younger members of Baron von Frankenfeld's family. When I told them that as a girl I could jump onto a horse without a saddler and, holding on to its mane, gallop through the fields, I immediately gained respect in their eyes. Soon, they were entrusting me with their best riding horses and even letting me use their gig if I wanted to make a shopping trip into the next town. In those days there were not many cars out in the country. It would be some years before we bought bicycles, after we moved to our next place.

Well, I was tall, young, and slender. Pappa said I made an elegant figure sitting high up on a horse, with my blond hair flying in the wind. Despite his great love for animals and nature, he did not have great affection for these large, temperamental beasts. They were too unpredictable for him. But he knew that I could handle them. "Just look at your wife, Herr Zimmermann," the Baron's son shouted from a distance. It was one of those crisp East Prussian spring days. "Your wife is dashing away like a true Amazon!" What a nice compliment! I thought. But when Pappa talked about it later, I noticed sparks of jealousy in his eyes, mixed with his obvious proud. He could count on my faithfulness. Still, it is sometimes useful to keep men on their toes so that they don't come to take one for granted.

Soon I also won the respect of the Baron's coachmen and stable boys, who frequently called me over to the estate when they had trouble training temperamental young horses. I knew how to talk with them, at first with a strong yet loving voice, and they seemed to feel my will power. One day the boys laughed as they pointed to a black stallion. "Frau Teacher," they said, "No one up to now has been able to stay on his back for longer than a minute." Without hesitation I took up their challenge. The clever animal tried to get me off its back by moving sideways and rubbing its body against the side of the barn. I was faster, however. I dug my spurs into its sides, and off we galloped through the open gate into the freshly ploughed fields. Some of the hands working the furrows saw us coming, crossed themselves, and ran away. As the receptive earth soon tired the stallion out, he slowed down and became calm. Soaked in sweat, huffing and puffing, "my boy," now in a dance-like trot, had turned back, obviously eager to get home to his water source. *Nein*, it was not easy to throw me out of the saddle!

Ja, Mutti, I can still see the triumph flashing in your eyes whenever you told us this story. Not only you but all the people in your past come to life again in front of my mind's eye in these quiet hours as do the beautiful fields and forests of our lost homeland. Then I remember the

old East Prussian song,

> *Land of dark forests and crystal-clear lakes,*
> *Where wondrous light falls across spacious fields,*
> *While the ocean roars forth the chorale of time,*
> *And the great elks on shore listen to eternity.**

---

*The former German province of Ostpreussen [East Prussia] was separated from Danzig (Gdansk) to the West by the Weichsel River. To the north lay the Baltic Sea and the Baltic States of Latvia, Lithuania, and Estonia. Due east was Russia and due south, Poland. After World War II, the victorious Allies divided East Prussia into two parts, with the northern half which contained the warm-water harbor of Koenigsberg (now Kaliningrad)—the hometown of philosopher Immanuel Kant—going to the then Soviet Union, and the southern half to Poland.

2

My Early Years, 1931—1934

Birth

I was born Hannelore Elfriede Margarethe Zimmermann March 4, 1931, in the hospital wing of an old Crusader castle in the town of Roessel, East Prussia—at the time the northeastern most part of the German Reich.* My ancestors had settled in that region after the Reformation from different parts of Europe as a result of their persecution as Protestants at the hands of the Catholic majority. The King of Prussia, Frederick the Great, had been a student and friend of Voltaire and was dedicated to religious tolerance. For the most part, Protestants, Catholics, and Jews lived peacefully in our part of the world until Hitler began stirring things up in the years following my birth.

My delivery, according to my mother, was not easy, since I was not positioned correctly inside her uterus. In

---

* Since the final letter "ee" in German is pronounced something like the English "eh," my three given names had three or four syllables each. As I grew up, I was called "Lore" or the diminutive "Lorchen," though in school and other formal settings, "Hannelore" was always used. Later as an aupère in England, I acquired the nickname "Lolly." Several years after immigrating to America and marrying Reynold Feldman, I took the name "Simone," which is why a book about "Hannelore Zimmermann" has been written by "Simone Feldman."

those days in East Prussia, c-sections were not routinely performed and so it was not unusual for the mother and baby in such cases to die in childbirth. Fortunately, a good doctor saved both Mutti's life and mine. A devout Catholic, he was in prayer the whole time he massaged Mutti's belly in the ultimately successful effort to turn me head down. Since Mutti was too exhausted to breastfeed me, the patient nuns carried me around, a screaming little bundle, all night long, as they tried to get me to take the bottle. Apparently I was not too eager to enter this world. After the delivery, we were kept in the hospital for several weeks until Mutti and I were strong enough to go home.

Nor were my first days of life blessed with mild spring weather. Going home in a horse-drawn sled, we were surrounded by walls of snow from a recent storm that had come down from the Russian steppes. Cold and tired, Mutti was disappointed that she had produced another girl and not the boy she and Pappa had been hoping for. Less than nine years later, however, when World War Two began, she changed her mind when she realized her daughters, unlike sons, would not have to become soldiers to kill or be killed.

First Conscious Impressions

Sounds come from Mutti's lips:

Lieber Gott, mach mich fromm,
Dass ich in den Himmel komm.

Dear God, give me faith
That I enter Heaven's gates.

In the beginning there is the word God. I have no question, no doubt. It is all so natural and obvious. I feel so close to the Source. All is well.

In the Village

I am standing in a beautiful place. The sunlight is warming my body. I feel happy. There is our house. I am in a garden with big trees and bright flowers. There are all kinds of delightful animals which I pet and feed. Birds are singing, and the sky is blue.

I am in a room. In the corner stands a large wooden box which produces lovely sounds. They make me move and swing my body. I tiptoe lightly around. I hum and sing, trying to copy the words and voices. I feel very happy.

We are taking a long car ride to a place with lots and lots of people. Loud marching music fills the air. I am sitting high up on Pappa's shoulders and can look out across the sea of hat-covered heads in front of me. Then a large box carried by uniformed men and covered with a flag and a flower wreath passes by and disappears into the crowd. All the men around us have taken off their hats and look very sad. Many people cry. After a while I fall asleep in the warm sunshine only to wake up again at home. (Years later I learn that this was the funeral procession for Field Marshall von Hindenburg in the town of Tannenberg, where a memorial for this great hero of East Prussia and Germany had recently been erected.)

My third birthday is my first clear memory. After I wake up, Mutti takes me downstairs into Pappa's room, which was called the Master's Room [*Herrenzimmer*]. We children were allowed to enter it only on special occasions like holidays or when we had guests. There was a little, round table. On it in the middle were flickering candles. Round about were placed a bowl of candies, a piece of chocolate, a storybook and—best of all—a small toy car. Pappa, Mutti, and my sister Gerda were all smiles as they wished me a happy birthday and we kissed each other.

"There is a key that you wind up to make the car go," Pappa explained and showed me how to do it. Then off the car goes, landing underneath the big sofa. I crawl over to retrieve it, but Peter the cat—nobody had noticed him before—is faster than me. No doubt thinking the little toy is a mouse, he hits my cheek with his paw, bites the car, then runs away disappointed. I cry. Mutti wipes the blood from my face. One can clearly see the scratch in the flash picture Pappa took that afternoon when we had a little party with cake with Gerda and her friend Adelheid Napierski.

3

The Bird Funeral

Outside the house I meet other children. They want to play, but they also tell stories about battles that had taken place here in the last big war (two new words for me) and point to the many dark crosses in the fenced-in yard across from our house. There are many similar fenced-in yards with crosses at each end of the village. They throw shadows across my paradise.

I learn that people are buried underneath those crosses, and suddenly I know what death is. For a moment a dark cloud seems to cover everything, and I experience fear. I want my mommy to hold me now. Many nights follow when I wake up sobbing. Only Mutti can help by singing me back to sleep.

I learn that the place where we live is called Kaltenborn. (The Russian writer Alexander Solzhenitsyn mentions this village in his book *1914*.) My older sister, Gerda, asks the neighborhood children to help me overcome my recent shock by picking up dead animals like birds and holding funerals, complete with make-believe priests, processions, and prayers in a made-up language. (One of the boys based this language on the Latin he had heard at a real funeral in a Catholic church.) Dead things have to be buried, I learn, but life goes on.

One sunny summer afternoon, we go to even greater lengths with our rite. Having a procession and a "priest" is not enough. Someone is pointing to the big bell hanging in an open attic on top of the schoolhouse where our family lives. Real funerals always have church bells. The opportunity to sneak upstairs could not have been better, since our parents along with half the village are lined up on the main street to watch a column of cars pass. An older boy tells us the name of an important government official—Rudolf Hess—who is to lead the cars to the nearby World War I Heroes Cemetery. This is a big event for the villagers, since, besides the Post bus that goes from town to town, motor vehicles are rarely seen in our streets.

A boy called Horst, finding the moment suitable, enters the schoolhouse staircase. In no time the sound of the bell fills the air as we children march slowly along the garden path, singing our made-up hymn.

Suddenly, the solemnity of the moment is interrupted. "Fire! Fire!" The crowd in the next street shouts. "The schoolhouse is burning!" Fire! Fire!" Soon men and women with buckets of water are running into our front yard. They vainly look for signs of flames. "How dare you ring the school bell!" Mutti screams. "It's not a toy. It is only meant to be used as a fire alarm." Her next sentence is swallowed up by the sound of the approaching fire truck. Our playmates disappear through the bushes, leaving Gerda and me to stare dumbfounded at all the people suddenly surrounding us. Pappa takes us into the house. He does not scold us but only says not to do something like that again. I see a trace of a smile on his lips.

For weeks the villagers talked about how our funeral had upstaged the solemn visit of Rudolf Hess. But from then on, playing funeral lost its glow for us, and the practice gradually ceased.

4

Three Against One

t's summer 1935. I have just turned four that March. Every summer Pappa invites the Hank sisters, Dorle and Lotte, to come stay with us. Their parents, who own a large Rosenthal china store in a town called Bischofsstein, are friends of our parents. The Hanks are happy to give their girls a summer in the country while getting some free time for themselves. The girls are closer to my sister Gerda in age—five years older than me. So of course I enjoy hanging around with the big girls, which the three of them more or less tolerate. I only get upset with them when they take away my favorite toys, especially my big doll Ursel and her carriage, Christmas presents from my godmother, Tante Grete. In exchange they give me a ragged old teddy bear in a carton with a pull string connected to it, all of which is much prettier than Arschel ["Little Ass"] and her silly carriage, they tell me.

After a while when I try to reclaim my pretty doll, they laugh and say she is as ugly as the dirtiest woman in the village. I feel helpless. There are three of them, and they are all bigger. But they have gone too far. Gerda at least should be on my side. She is my sister after all. I brood about this situation for days. One day at lunch, when my hurt feelings are about to suffocate me, I suddenly get up from my chair, calmly put down my spoon, go over to my sister's place, and slap her as hard as I can on the cheek.

Gerda screams. My parents look at each other,

speechless. "What is going on here? Why did you do that, Lorchen?" Pappa asks. Meantime Mutti, clearly angry, is trying to calm my sister down. After describing the situation, I say this is the only thing I can do to defend myself, since the other girls are bigger and stronger than me. Even if Mutti and Pappa punish me, I want them to see how I feel.

My parents take Gerda to the other room and talk with her. From then on, she leaves me in peace. Dorle and Lotte change their behavior too. They are nice girls after all, and I have always liked them.

5

My First Attempt to Swim

Pappa would often take me on bike rides when I was small. I would enjoy sitting in the little seat up front as he pedaled through the village and the adjoining forest to the beautiful, round lake in the midst of pine trees. There are even some benches for the adults and a white sand beach there, the recent effort of a school class. On the way he would regale me with stories, like the one about the dwarves who come out of their hollowed-out oak-tree homes at night to paint the berries. How fantastic! I of course believe every word.

It is fun playing in the water with my big sister and her friends. When they try taking me into deeper water to teach me how to swim, though, I resist vigorously and even begin to panic. Why? I also scream when Mutti pours too much water over my head during the evening bath. Why should that be so frightening?

One night when I am five, I have a vivid dream. I am sitting in the sand with a little bucket and shovel. In front of me are Mutti's long legs, spread apart like a gate through which I see the rippling water. "Be a good girl and stay put," I hear her saying. But my whole attention is focused on a group of children, including my sister, who are splashing and laughing as they play with some kind of wooden wheel. Next to them I see Pappa in his black bathing suit watching them. Suddenly I am overwhelmed by the wish to be with them. Before I know it, I am throwing myself with full force into the water. Then I can

27

see nothing. From far away I hear Pappa's voice: "Where is Lore? Where is Lore?"

Waking with a start, I run into my parents' room and climb into Mutti's bed. Trembling and hugging her tightly, I relate my frightening dream. Finally, I fall asleep again.

The next morning at breakfast, with sunlight flooding the room and banishing the fright of my nightmare, Mutti tells me that what I dreamed had actually happened. It was when I was two years old and we were still living in Worplack. "Now that you have re-lived this experience in a dream, it is 'out,' and you will be freed of your anxiety about water. You see, *mein Liebes* [my dear], this is what can happen if you don't obey your mother," she adds with a affirming smile.

"But I was only a baby," I say. "You should have watched me better!"

` "That's true," Mutti responds, "but following my orders is still very difficult for you, isn't it?"

"Tell me, Mutti, who pulled me out of the water? Someone must have, because I'm still here, alive."

"For that you have your father to thank. In the split second that I turned to look at the playing children, I heard him calling your name, then jumping forward and pulling your little body out of the muddy pond. You had been doggie-paddling downward. Fortunately, Pappa saw your bald head through the murky water, grabbed you by one of your legs, and pulled you up. By that point you had stopped breathing. Pappa shook you but to no avail. Suddenly out of nowhere a young man appeared who was able to knock the water out of your lungs. No one knew who he was, and he disappeared as quickly as he had come.

"What? I was bald?" I said in a quivering voice. "Only old *Opas* [grandpas] are bald!" What could be more insulting to a five-year-old girl? Hot tears stream down my checks. Trying to reassure myself, I clutch my pigtails with both hands.

"What, my child? Are you going to cry again? You should know that it was your bald head that kept you from drowning. On the advice of our barber, we had your head shaved that summer. He thought doing so would cause your fine hair to grow back stronger."

With an encouraging nod and a smile, Mutti ends our conversation. Clearing the table with a swift movement, she disappears into the kitchen. After fumbling for a little while with my pigtails, I am off into the young summer day to see what adventures might lurk around the corner.

After this dream I overcame my fear of the water and learned how to swim. Swimming in fact became my favorite exercise, which it remains to this day, some 70 years later.

6

My First Experience of Christmas

Kaltenborn, East Prussia. Advent 1934. I am three going on four. It is the first Christmas Season I remember

Mutti tells Gerda and me about Advent, the time of preparation for the birth of the Christ Child, the special one sent by God. She places a green pine wreath decorated with red ribbons and four candles beneath the large lamp in our living room. "Every Sunday we shall light one new candle until Christmas Day comes. So be good children, otherwise Nicklaus [St. Nicholas, Santa Claus] may not bring you any presents." When daylight fades, we sit by the flickering candles while Mutti teaches us sweet Advent hymns. It is so warm and cozy inside. Outside, cold winds howl.

Today something special is going on. Our house is part of the school building where Pappa serves as village schoolmaster. For some reason the doors to the classrooms are wide open. Lots of children walk back and forth. They are chatting and laughing. It all seems so exciting. I follow them. A few women with Mutti in the lead are busy with rolls of white paper and piles of white material which they are wrapping around some of the children. This cannot be a regular class session, because it is not morning. Outside, the bluish light of evening colors the snowy fields.

I watch as Mutti puts an enormous red paper hat with white polka dots on the head of one of the boys. "You are a mushroom," she tells him. "And you will be a pine tree," she tells another as she places a huge green paper bag, cut in a zigzag design, over his body. And so it goes until a whole forest has been created.

She next puts a girl and a boy in the midst of all the costumed children. She calls them Haensel [Hansel] and Gretel. "Hurry up, you little Snowflakes. We have to practice your dance one more time." A group of girls, dressed in white lacy outfits, quickly form a circle around the pair. In the background the other children begin singing

> *Little snowflake, little snowflake,*
> *When will you come down?*
> *With your little white skirt*
> *You live up in the cloud*
> *So very far away.*

All at once, the circle begins to move. Arms form arches through which the Snowflakes take turns gliding back and forth. Then they tiptoe to the center and back to narrow and widen the circle. After a while, the Snowflakes separate and whirl quickly to the side and off the stage area. Suddenly two girls collide and fall down. "You dumb cow," one yells. "Pay attention!" "No. It's all your fault!" The other shouts back. Then, they each hold their heads and cry like crazy. "Come on, girls. Stop that! It's not all that bad. Everything will be fine by the time you get married," I hear Mutti tell them.

"Come on. Let's try it again," she adds. "This time I want you all to be perfect little ballerinas." Then she motions to me. "Come over here, child, and join us." She doesn't have to ask twice. The whole time I was watching, my heart was burning with the desire to take part. It does

31

not matter that I don't have a white dress like the others. I know how to dance and am absolutely convinced that I can do it better than the larger girls. Without a moment's hesitation, I jump into the circle and forget everything else that is going on. I am all dance. What happiness!

Years later Mutti told me that from the time I learned to walk, I always went on tiptoes, with the result that the fronts of all my pretty shoes were scratched. She thought there might be something wrong with my feet, so she took me to a doctor. He only laughed and said that I would outgrow this peculiar habit in due course. Little did he know that for me, to walk on tiptoes meant to dance.

Anyway, the day of the performance finally arrives. It is Saturday afternoon. Our house is abuzz with activities—packing up costumes, painted stage sets, and the like. To keep us away from the commotion, Gerda and I are sent to the kitchen where Christel, our new helper in the house, gives us something to eat. We poke around absentmindedly at our food. We are too excited to eat. We look out the big kitchen window as everything is loaded onto the great horse-drawn wagon. It will take its load to Gasthof Naht. There, on the stage of the grand ballroom, the Christmas play will take place.

My heart is pounding faster and faster. Waiting is so hard. The afternoon seems endless. Finally the big moment arrives. The two of us and Christel enter the large, noisy hall. We wind our way through the throngs of people to chairs in the first row. It is reserved for the family members of the cast. Before I know it, Gerda has disappeared through one of the stage doors. There are two, one on either side of the stage. Mutti emerges from the other. She comes straight to me and says, "Now listen, child. You stay on Christel's lap until I call you. Do you understand?" "Ja, Mutti," I respond. "Meanwhile, you can sit here and enjoy the First Act." I nod and wait impatiently for the curtain to rise.

To pass the time, I watch the orchestra, just in front of us. At the moment they are producing awful screeching sounds. They all wear neat black suits, white shirts buttoned at the neck, and funny black butterflies made of cloth on their collars. The musicians are all from the village. I recognize some of them. There is the butcher, Herr Matern, daintily playing the flute with his thick fingers. Then there is the bony-faced tailor, Herr Rausch, who is hitting a board with two little hammers. After him I see Herr Kowalski, the black-haired photographer, who is playing the trumpet. I remember how he took such a long time taking our family photograph that I ended up with an angry expression that pretty much ruined the picture. Next is the friendly forester, Herr Engelhardt, with his wavy brown hair. He is playing an instrument that looks like Opa's long pipe. Near him sits *Friseur* [hair dresser] Schmilewski with his neatly parted, oily hair. Holding a violin under his double chin, he fiddles so vigorously that pearls of sweat appear on his forehead. Last but not least, I recognize the fat farmer, Herr Maier, with his red hair. As big as he is, he seems to disappear behind his huge trumpet, which Pappa calls a tuba. He blows with such force that I am afraid he will pop all the buttons on his tightly fitting suit. With his bulging eyes and cheeks, he reminds me of an oversized bullfrog.

When will the show begin? I wonder. The whole thing is taking too long for me. Finally, Pappa comes out of the stage door on the left and walks to the piano, where the Deaconess Luise awaits him on the bench. Turning to the audience before he sits down, he announces in a loud voice that the Community Christmas Celebration will begin with the *"Petersburger Schlittenfahrt"* ["Petersburg Sleigh Ride"]. After he places himself next to Frau Luise, the two of them begin to play. Their four hands race back and forth over the black and white keys. It is such a joyful piece of music that everyone applauds enthusiastically at the end.

Suddenly the lights dim, and the curtain finally opens. Eagerly I absorb the First Act, although I have my own critical thoughts about the bread crumbs which Haensel and Gretel scatter on their path in order to find their way home. The birds and the other forest animals could eat them, for example. Wouldn't it be better for the children to keep their food for later? They may have a long trek ahead of them.

For a few moments they walk to and fro across the stage. In the end, they disappear behind Mutti's pine trees and mushrooms, only to reappear and move toward the front of the stage. The musicians meantime produce soft, chirping sounds like those of birds. The children stop in the middle of the stage under a tall fir tree, a real one donated by Forester Engelhardt, where they lie down to sleep, their heads resting on their bread bags. Suddenly two big angels in flowing white gowns enter the scene. Wearing shining gold wreaths on their heads and accompanied by the orchestra, they sing the most beautiful lullaby I have ever heard. My eyes fill up with tears, and everything becomes a blur.

Soon, though, I can see clearly again. And what do I see but the Snowflakes taking up their positions on stage as the orchestra begins to play the familiar song! O God! I think. Why has no one called me? Where is Mutti? She promised! This is all wrong! I am part of the dancers! Without a moment to lose, I jump down from Christel's lap and climb over the knees and shoulders of the dumbfounded musicians, who have difficulty holding on to their instruments, let alone playing. I don't care. I feel so betrayed. They have forgotten me!

From the last shoulder I swing my right leg onto the stage, grab a hand, and am suddenly part of the circle. Why do the girls give me such a strange look? Didn't I come in at the right time? Joyfully I glide around the stage as if on wings. Laughter suddenly bubbles forth from the audience. Why? Can't they see that this is a very serious performance? Each time I turn to face the audience, my expression becomes angrier. When I finally throw my head back in sheer disgust, the audience roars with laughter and explodes into applause.

Without a word to anyone, I leave the stage after the dance and stagger back to where Christel is sitting. Climbing onto her lap, I put my head on her shoulder. "Let's go—I want to get out of here," I say. "Christel, I have to go peepee!"

We hurry out of the still-darkened ballroom. I miss the Final Act, but I don't care. Mutti promised to call me but never did. A promise is a promise!

Christel and I wait for Mutti and Pappa in the lobby next to the ballroom. We are sitting at a little table. Our smiling host, Herr Naht, approaches and places a glass of lemonade in front of me. "Here is a little treat, my child, for the wonderful performance you gave. Everyone says that having you climb up onto the stage at the last minute was your father's best inspiration." My gaze is glued to the red-checkered tablecloth. My throat is tight and dry. Somehow I manage to squeeze out a quivering *Dankeschoen* [Thanks]. As I take a sip of the lemonade, hot tears fall into the glass. What does he know? I think.

Suddenly I am lifted from the chair and find myself seated high up on Pappa's broad shoulders. Before I know it, we are back in the ballroom, where tables and chairs have been spread around for the remaining guests to enjoy Herr Naht's food and drink. Pappa gives me a piece of chocolate. Sitting in his lap, I calm down and begin to feel better. In front of him is a large glass of beer with a big crown of foam on top. It looks so inviting that while he is chatting with the person next to him, I try a sample. "Yuck, is that bitter!" I exclaim.

"Hi, Lorchen [diminutive of Lore in German], where did you get that white mustache?" A voice close to me says. "Would you like to come onto my lap for a little while? I have a nice Gretel doll made of chocolate for you because you were such a beautiful dancer up there." A bony hand points to the now-deserted stage. Ach, it's the *Arbeitsdeinstfueher* [Nazi Work Brigade leader] Schiefelbein with his wide grin. Whenever he marches his trainees past our schoolhouse, he has them sing "Lore, Lore, Lore" in my honor. According to this folk song, only girls between 17 and 18 are beautiful. *Na, so was!* [Give me a break!] What a dumb idea!

Neither his encouraging grin nor the chocolate Gretel has any effect on me. "*Nein. Dankeschoen.* I'd rather stay with Pappa." My father mumbles something about the late hour, all the excitement, and how overtired I must be, then turns to engage Herr Schiefelbein in conversation. Pappa suggests that the Arbeitsdeinst consider building a home for the family of the poor lumberjack Napierski and his eight children. (Two of them are my friends.) "The project would be a change of pace for the boys," Pappa offers, "after all the time they've spent clearing swamps. I am sure Herr Nowotka [the owner of the village sawmill] would be happy to donate some building materials. Then the boys could go home at the end of the summer with the feeling of having done a good deed for a poor *Volksgenossen* [Brother German; literally, "People's comrade"], whose children are intelligent and well behaved—something I can attest to as their teacher."

I never heard the rest of the conversation because at that point Mr. Sandman had done his work. Not only did I fall asleep, but when I woke up, my hurt feelings had disappeared.

Afterthought

I remember that two years later, after we had moved to a new place, we received a letter with a family photo. It showed a proud Napierski family with contented smiles in front of their new wooden house. Unfortunately, their happiness did not last long. Only a few years later, their eldest sons were killed in World War II as paratroopers in Greece, and by 1945 their house along with the other houses in the village was totally destroyed. As with so many, we never found out what became of the other family members in the course of the War.

7

An Incomplete Gift of Pansies

After a long, snowy winter, complete with icy winds, I am happy to see green meadows again, filled with buttercups and other types of flowers. I am now four. Enthusiastically I run down the little hill behind our house. In my eagerness I disregard the surface mud that stains my shoes and socks. As soon as I can, I throw myself down on my back in the green splendor. Looking up, I watch as white cotton-ball-like clouds drift slowly across the blue vastness of the May sky. All is well.

Mutti is not so sure. When she sees my soiled clothing, she sends me to bed after lunch. This isn't exactly a punishment. She usually has me take a nap. Still, this is something I really don't enjoy. Afternoon naps seem such a waste. There is so much to see and do outside. So, most of the time, instead of sleeping, I look out my second-floor window at the birds flying from tree to tree. I listen to their chirping and marvel at their different-colored feathers. But today I am absorbed in thought. Mutti was really upset by how dirty I got. How can I make it up to her? Maybe I can bring her a nice bunch of flowers, as Pappa sometimes does. She always seems so happy when he does that.

When naptime is over, I rush downstairs and out into the backyard. What a surprise! Next to the long side of the house I find bunches of pretty flowers in yellow, blue, white, and purple. They all have little faces which look up invitingly at me as if to say, "We are the answer to your problem."

I waste no time. One by one they each land in my new white apron. At that very moment I hear my parents' voices as they round the corner from the front yard. Eagerly I rush toward them and smilingly spread my apron out in front of Mutti. "Look, Mutti," I exclaim excitedly, "I brought you a gift!" Mutti frowns, and in a second my smile disappears. Turning to Pappa, she says, "Look, Hans, at what our Little Miss Mischief has done. She has gone and torn out all the pansies we just planted!"

Noticing the tears welling up in my eyes, her features soften. She kneels down and strokes my hand. Then she picks up one of the pansies and begins to teach me how to pick flowers. "Lorchen, don't pick just the heads," she explains. "You have to go down the stem of each flower with your fingers until you reach the ground. Then you pluck it. That way the flowers you pick can stand in a vase." Still sulking, I nod my head. This is one of the first lessons I remember my mother giving me.

I was wrong as an adult to think she had forgotten this incident. A lifetime later in 1990 when I visited her in Saint Joseph's Hospital, Saint Paul, where she spent her last days, a film of her life seemed to be running through her head. She turned to me at one point and said, "I just saw you standing next to my bed as a four-year-old with the pansy faces in your apron. Pappa and I had just planted those flowers. You were some little rascal!"

I couldn't interrupt her. A mother now myself, I knew how eager small children are to please their parents and how we grownups sometime misinterpret their attempts to show us their love. Our world is not theirs.

But the story doesn't end here. The day before Mutti's memorial service, my friend Lailani showed up on our doorstep with a single large purple-and-white pansy. I had never told her this story. The next day at the open-casket celebration of Mutti's life, I placed this correctly picked pansy on her hand. The gift was now complete.

8

Bringing Home Dinner

f it was too cool to go to the lake, Pappa would take us on extended walks in the surrounding forest. Along the way he would teach us the names of the different trees, plants, berries, and mushrooms, making sure we could distinguish the poisonous from the non-poisonous kinds. He also pointed out the different animals that lived in the forest and explained about their habitats. Sometimes the Leidereither family would accompany us.

Mid-summer was the perfect time to gather wild strawberries and blueberries. Mutti, Gerda, and I would join the village women as they looked for these delicacies. The first time I can remember, I was still quite small. They put me with my little tin bucket in the midst of a field full of wild blueberries. What joy! Naturally, more berries landed in my mouth than in the bucket. By the time Mutti came to get me, her little girl was entirely blue. It took days to wash all the color from my face, neck, and hands.

Often we gathered so many berries that Mutti made several large berry tarts. For our evening meal we children ate sugared blueberries or strawberries in fresh milk accompanied by dark bread covered with country butter. Nothing tasted better than wild berries and dark bread. What a feast!

When the leaves of the white birch trees lining the edge of the forest turned golden red and the first formations of wild geese flew over our house, I knew that the warm days would soon be over. I learned that this time of year was called autumn. In the evening you could hear the distant roars of fighting stags—a sound that seemed quite sad and gloomy.

Fortunately, there were still plenty of sunny days for playing outside. One morning when I was about to feed the chickens from a large bowl Mutti had given me, I overheard her say to herself, "I have no idea what to cook for dinner today." (Back in East Prussia when I was growing up, we ate our main meal—dinner—at noontime.) "I know—I know!" I thought. Disregarding the big yellow hen who was sitting expectantly near my feet, I set my bowl down and stole out of the yard. I ran as fast as I could toward the woods nearby where I knew I would find the edible little yellow mushrooms. They tasted so good when Mutti fried them with onions.

To my joy, I found plenty, and in no time my apron was filled to the top. Soon I was back in the kitchen and, with a proud smile, presented my harvest to a flabbergasted mother. I knew by her smile that this time I had done something right and was overjoyed when she gave me a big hug. Later she told me that she and Gerda had spent an hour looking for me in the neighborhood. Well, I guess I still had something to learn about doing things totally right.

9

The Injured Stork

O n one of those sunny fall days, something surprising and wonderful happens. Farmer Maier appears in our front yard with a large, wiggling object under his arm. It turns out to be a big bird with a long, red beak.

"Herr Teacher, do you have any idea what we can do with this poor stork? I found him in my potato field. He obviously has a broken wing and will never be able to continue his migration south this year. As you can see, he is a special bird, since on his left foot there is a silver ring marked 'Bird Sanctuary Rossitten.'"

Pappa nods. "That is a place on the north of the Kurische Nehrung [a peninsula jutting out into the Baltic Sea, in the extreme northeast of East Prussia]. I'll inform them that the bird is here, and we will take care of him until his wing is healed. My wife knows how to bandage him with a wooden splint underneath the wing."

Farmer Maier's mouth drops open, and with an awkward expression he asks, "But how will you take care of him all winter long, Herr Teacher?"

"Simple! We'll make room for him in the barn with the other animals. My children, the school children, and I will gather food from the meadows and see what we can get from the butcher. If poultry is slaughtered in the village, the children can ask for the entrails. We can all learn from this experience."

"Sure, sure," Maier stammers. "But tell me where I can put him now." "This way," Pappa replies, and the two men walk off toward our barn.

The stork stays there for some time. We children love watching him get fed. Whenever something edible is brought to him, he dances around, throws his long, white neck backwards, and makes a clapping sound with his beak in anticipation of the meal to come.

One day the director of the *Arbeitsdeinst* Camp in Kaltenborn, Emil Rabe, hears about our unusual guest and stops by with a proposition for Pappa. "Herr Teacher, my recruits and I can gather plenty of food for your stork from the swamps we clear, and, if you like, we can give him a more spacious home in our camp."

Pappa agrees, and the stork becomes the Camp's mascot for the rest of the winter. When the weather turns milder, the bird is given his freedom to wander around the exercise grounds. The next thing we children know, there he is, marching alongside the young Work Corps troupers in their columns. The stork is a great source of fun for the boys. Then, one sunny spring day, Mr. Stork feels that his wing is strong enough and it is time to go home. Flapping confidently, he rises high above the camp to the cheers of the boys. As if to show his appreciation for the good care he has received, he slowly circles the camp grounds three times before heading north and vanishing from sight.

Weeks later Pappa receives a letter from the Bird Sanctuary in Rossitten. Our bird has arrived safely. They confirm the number on his silver ring and thank Pappa and the village for their help. We are all delighted and relieved.

❖

10

The Cat Baptism

That same spring, Pappa built a little caged enclosure for rabbits. He called it "Long Ear Village." Along with it came a new white, fluffy pet for me, which I named Hansi. He followed me around everywhere and even slept next to me on the grass. In addition, there was Peter the cat, who preferred sleeping next to my doll Ursel on the white cushions of my doll carriage.

Muschi, our other cat, showed up one day with a new litter of four kittens in tow. Gerda and I gave them names but felt the need to baptize them as well, together with Peter, who was already an older cat.

As god parents we asked Heidi Napierski and Helga Leidereither, the local policeman's daughter, who was Gerda's friend. One of Heidi's older brothers agreed to serve as pastor. (No, there would be no bell-ringing this time!)

From our birthdays all of us girls had tiny red-nippled bottles filled with pearl-like candies. Shaking out the candies, we filled these bottles with milk to feed the kittens. The latter we wrapped in a little blanket to keep them quiet and content during the ceremony. Holding the bottles with their front paws and sucking happily, they did not even mind getting sprinkled with water. But when it came time to baptize Peter, clad in a long, white doll's dress and lying purring on a white cushion in my arms, he jumped high up into the air at the first drop of Holy Water and with a great spring reached a nearby cherry tree. Before we knew it, he had climbed to the top. Left behind on the branches were small, torn remnants of the pretty white dress. This then was the grand finale of our cat baptism.

These were the days long before TV. In fact, most of the neighbor children didn't even have a radio. We had to invent our own games and create other ways to entertain ourselves. Maybe this is the reason my childhood memories are so clearly preserved. My mind was not yet polluted by the many competing images from the flickering screen.

But life in the country back then was not all sunshine and roses either. The older I grew, the more aware I became of some disturbing sights and sounds around the neighborhood. There were the terrible shrieks of a pig being slaughtered, the loud cursing of a drunk stumbling home, or the sight of a headless roster in its last vain attempt to escape from the farmer's hands. It was in these days that I vowed not to eat any more meat.

11

My Relatives

When Pappa had summer vacation, my grandparents—Opa Ernst, Oma Lina, and Oma Dorchen (as we called her)—as well as other visitors like Great Aunt Frieda (a sister of Opa Ernst), Pappa's brother Uncle Erich, and other family relatives and friends came to visit for a few days and sometimes for weeks. Opa Ernst was a quiet, friendly man, very tall, with a little mustache. Whenever he came, he fixed whatever was broken in the house. Old photos from his youth showed him with a Kaiser Wilhelm mustache. I liked him a lot but didn't like to be kissed by him, since his mustache scratched my checks. Though he understood my reason, it still made him sad, but he never shaved his mustache.

Oma Lina was fun. She knew how to play games that a four-year-old like me would like. We would take naps together, and she would tell me about her own childhood. The sudden death of her mother was the great tragedy of her early years. She was only eight when her mother died in childbirth. "Always be good to your mother," she told me, "because no one can replace a mother's love." Those words had a big impact on me.

When she spoke, I noticed that her teeth shifted around. "What's the matter with your teeth, Oma?" I burst out one day. Curious as I was, I reached into her open mouth and pulled out her upper bridge. Oma was not pleased. "You little imp," she shouted. Give me those back at once!" We both laughed so hard that the tears rolled down our cheeks. Then she wagged her index finger at me. "Don't ever do that again! Understand?"

Oma Dorchen, Pappa's mother, was a serene woman, if a bit distant. She had been the only girl in her family and had raised only boys—Pappa and Uncle Erich. A third son had died in infancy. She did not have the right touch for girls, Mutti said. (Mutti in fact was pretty critical of Oma Dorchen.) However, Oma must have done a good job with her boys, because they adored her and always called her Mamachen, "Little Mommy." Not only was this a term of endearment, but it was descriptive too. Compared with her sons, she was tiny.

Whenever Tante Frieda would visit from Neidenburg, her nearby hometown, we kids had a good time. She had lost her only child in infancy and, to make up for this loss, Mutti told us, she would spend a lot of time with us. She was a tall, handsome woman. In her youth, it was said, she was the beauty of Neidenburg with her big blue eyes and long blond braids. When I first remember her, her hair was short and styled in the fashion of the Thirties. Her clothes were always chic—cleverly chosen to conceal her rather prominent hips. She had a peculiar way of ending nearly all her sentences with the phrase "You know?" *["Na nicht?"]* As a result, we children nicknamed her Tante Na-Nicht, "Auntie You-Know." She would also lift her tea or coffee cups with her pinky sticking out. After she left, I would imitate her mannerisms down to walking like her, swinging my skinny hips as best I could. "Oh," Mutti would say. "Frieda thinks you are a nice, quiet little girl. Obviously, she hasn't seen this side of you yet!"

In the course of the year, when my parents wanted to take a break from us children, they would ship us off to Tante Frieda's place in Neidenburg. Divorced by this time, she was living with her aging parents, my great grandparents, Luise and Eduard Radtke, who by then were in their early 80's.

After Great Grandpa had made enough money in the brick business in Warsaw, Poland, he invested most of his assets in real estate on the south side of the Neidenburg castle. He had an old farmhouse converted into a country inn. Next to it he planted a large flower and vegetable garden which adjoined an expansive meadow. When we played there, Gerda and I could see, not far away, the castle surrounded by tall trees. It was like a fairytale picture come to life.

I can remember Great Grandma Luise. She was a tall, slender woman with a kind face. Though in her 80's, she would stand each day in the kitchen, cooking the most delicious meals. Tante Frieda, meanwhile, took care of the household duties and oversaw the business.

Besides Frieda, there was another daughter in the house—Tante Lieschen, a small, shy woman with a hunchback caused by a childhood fall. Apparently the effect of the injury had been detected too late to prevent her deformity. Unable to do much physical work, she had learned embroidery and needlepoint and produced the most beautiful work. She even earned a good bit of money through her handicraft, mostly by monogramming dowry linen. She had beautiful dark-blond hair that reached to her knees. I would watch fascinated each morning as she brushed and then twisted it into a knot which she pinned up at the back of her head.

One day someone shoved a newspaper under the front door. I picked it up to bring it into the living room. With a shudder, I quickly threw it back to the ground. There on the front page was a large, ugly picture of a man with a long, crooked nose; penetrating, hawk-like eyes; and

49

oversized ears shaped like the number six. I picked the paper up again and brought it to Tante Lieschen. Looking up over the tops of her glasses from her needlework, she said, "We never ordered that paper." Then she shouted, "Frieda, someone has pushed the *Stuermer* [an anti-Semitic Nazi newspaper] under our door again. I guess they want to teach us what Jews are supposed to look like!"

This was the first time I had heard the word *Jew*. When I asked for an explanation, Tante Lieschen just said, "They are people who live among us and are not Christians, but none of them looks like that picture."

Tante Frieda, laughing, entered the room. "You weren't home last week, Lieschen, you know, when two Party people came to interrogate Father. They wanted to find out the names of all his ancestors and where they were from, you know. I suppose they doubted his Aryan lineage because of his beak-like nose!"

"They came from Bohemia in Austria," he told the Nazis, "and settled down after the Reformation in Stettin on the Baltic Sea." "When the interrogators asked him what kind of work they did, he gave them a dirty look, you know, and said, 'They were pirates!' Then he asked them 'Who put those little dwarves into that wooden box over there? They babble all day long and drive me crazy!' He pointed to our radio, you know. 'Well, Herr Radtke,' one of them answered with a big grin, 'you'd better let your daughter explain it to you.' Then they both stood up, you know, said 'Heil Hitler,' turned, and left."

From then on, Great Grandpa became more interesting to me. For the most part, he would sit clad in warm house shoes in the big armchair next to the oven. He did not move around much, Tante Frieda told me, because he was half blind and did not hear very well. He had beautiful silver-white hair, slightly curled, with a single soft strand falling over his high forehead. His eyes were light blue. "Poor Great Grandpa," I thought. "It must be hard to grow so old and become so limited in your activities." I watched him from a distance. There was something about him that kept me from ever getting too close. He always seemed so absorbed in his thoughts.

On a particular morning, one of Tante Frieda's big cats—she had four—was sleeping contentedly on his lap. I should note here that when it came to her cats, Tante Frieda was very protective. They were like her children. She even trained them like circus animals. On her command they would jump over sticks or through rings. When we ate lunch, moreover, they would sit beside us on cushions placed on the chairs to boost them up. With their front paws on the table, they would lick their food very neatly off special little plates. Mutti explained later that cats are very independent by nature and that only someone with an exceptionally strong will could train them. I was impressed. It was one of the many reasons I enjoyed visiting Tante Frieda.

Anyway, to get back to the story, on that particular day I observed Great Grandpa pulling out a little box from his jacket and pouring some white powder onto the back of his left hand. Lifting the hand to his nose, he sniffed the powder in. (Today's readers would probably think the substance was cocaine. Actually, it was snuff.) Then pouring out a little more—I couldn't believe my eyes!—he rubbed it on the cat's nose. Jumping up nearly to the ceiling, the crazed cat landed on the dining table. Whirling around wildly several times and meowing in panic, the cat sent the pretty tablecloth, vase, and flowers crashing to the floor, where they landed on Great Grandma's fancy Persian carpet. When Tante Frieda rushed into the room, I told her what had happened. Turning to Great Grandpa, she yelled, "You old fool! Why did you do that to that poor animal?" I had never heard her speak in such an angry voice before, especially to her own father. His body shook with laughter as he looked up at her with the expression of a schoolboy caught in a prank. I couldn't help smiling. For him it was all just a little private joke to spice up the monotony of his daily routine.

12

The 60th Anniversary

I n March 1935 we were invited to Neidenburg for a big event in my grandparents' house—a con-celebration of their 60th anniversary together with my parents' tenth. Tante Frieda had sent Gerda and me beautiful white muslin dresses with embroidery on top by Tante Lieschen. It was a cool spring day, and the church was not heated. Gerda and I insisted on preceding the old couple to the altar. More to the point, we refused any covering so that everyone could see our beautiful but not very warm dresses. "What vanity!" Mutti laughed, as we shivered our way down the aisle.

Fortunately, the service was short. Soon we were back at our grandparents' inn, where we were given cocoa while the adults toasted with other kinds of hot drinks. Soon a photographer arrived to take a group picture. After positioning the adults before the precious china cabinet, he told Gerda and me to stand in front of our great grandparents and look at each other. Curious however to see what the man was doing behind his big box, I moved my head and eyes slightly to the side. Of course, that was just the moment when the big flash explosion filled the room with light, preserving the scene forever—you can find the picture in this book. And there for the world to see was my impish independence, even as the four-year-old daughter of a country schoolmaster in 1930's East Prussia.

13

The Plum Tree

n summer my sister Gerda knew where to find all the edible things in Tante Frieda's garden—radishes, carrots, berries, and above all plums from the wonderful plum tree. There was a restriction, though. We were permitted to pick up fallen fruit only, since Great Grandma needed the whole harvest to preserve for the long winter or to bake into her cakes.

We of course thought the plums from the tree were much more delicious. So, when we couldn't find any in the grass, we helped some get there by shaking the tree. One day we were caught in the act, with the result that that part of the garden was closed off to us with a new locked gate. Nonetheless, Great Grandma had mercy on us and made sure we each got a daily ration of plums.

Fifty years later, when Gerda had the opportunity to visit our old homeland, now Poland, for the first and last time, she went to see what had become of Great Grandpa's place in Neidenburg. Besides the meadows and part of the garden, nothing was left. A new house had replaced his cozy inn. Only the old plum tree, roots firmly anchored in the soil, was still there. It made her cry.

14

Pappa

Most of the time Pappa was kind and considerate to us. Normally somewhat strict, he became quite firm and angry when we children attempted to tell a lie. One afternoon, for example, he watched from the kitchen window as Gerda took a gander by the neck, swung it around a few times, and released it in mid-air. The village children had told us that this was the only way to defend yourself against ganders which could become quite vicious and inflict a bad bite. In this case, the gander had hissed as it approached us, so Gerda followed the children's advice.

Later, when we re-entered the house, Pappa asked us where we had been and what we had been doing. "Oh, we were just playing in the garden," one of us replied. We both looked at the floor. "Is that all?" He asked scornfully. "Yes," we replied, our gaze still toward our feet.

"Do you call that playing when you torture an animal? I watched you. I saw everything!"

Shaking and with tears in our eyes, we tried to explain why Gerda had done what she did. His anger did not abate. Instead, he went to a corner of the kitchen where a thin walking stick was hanging. Giving us a stern look, he said, "I accept your explanation. You should have told me that in the first place. But I cannot tolerate your lying. Do you hear me? Cruelty to animals is bad too. I know you were afraid, but you followed poor advice. Next time keep your distance from the geese. They were only trying to protect their young."

"So, if I punish you now, it is because you told a lie. Remember, I will always listen to the truth, regardless of what it is. Things can always be talked out."

With that, he took down the walking stick and laid us over a kitchen chair, one after the other. Then he gave each of us a good whipping. When he had finished, he marched out of the kitchen and left us to Mutti for consolation. For days Gerda and I had red marks on our behinds and needed cushions to sit on a chair.

This was the old-fashioned way to mould a child's character. We sulked for a few days and did not speak, but we knew Pappa had taught us a lesson we would not soon forget. Children are very forgiving. They cling to their parents with all their love, because parents are the only stable thing they have.

15

Hallowe'en in Kaltenborn

round noon one Saturday in fall, Mutti asked me to go across the street to the Napierskis and ask if the two older daughters, Waltraud and Adelheid, could come over and spend the afternoon and evening with Gerda and me. It was a gray day with streaks of sunlight barely penetrating the fog. Since it was All Saints' Eve, Mutti had baked a batch of marmalade-filled donuts traditional for that Holiday. Our parents had been invited to take a car ride to Jablonken, the next village, to visit friends. They planned to be home by 10 p.m.

"Oh Ja," the Napierski girls readily agreed, and not just because of Mutti's donuts. They liked to play with us "in the teacher's house," which was so much roomier than the tiny apartment they shared with their parents and five siblings.

Their front room was a combination of kitchen, dining area, and sleeping quarters for the kids. Two long wooden beds lined the side walls. The three girls slept in one, while the four brothers, two of whom were still little, crowded into the other. Their parents occupied the small bedroom in the back.

When I came in, the family was sitting around a large table. In the middle stood a big bowl of boiled potatoes. Next to it was a smaller bowl containing some kind of soupy liquid. It turned out to be salt water from the herring barrel, which they got for free from the grocery store along with the herring or two they bought. The latter were divided into small pieces and placed back into the salt water. In this way, everyone could have a bite. Then, sticking their forks into the potatoes, they dipped them into the "sauce" and ate. Trying to conceal my shock at their meager meal, I waved my hand and said, "See you later." They looked content, smiled, and waved back.

In our living room, meanwhile, the dining table had been extended to make room for the four of us to sit comfortably. Mutti had provided enough paper, pencils, crayons, and card games to keep us occupied and entertained until she and Pappa returned. We all enjoyed drawing. We started by making portraits of each other. Not always flattering, they caused lots of giggles and laughter. "My nose is not that big!" "Yes it is!" "Your pigtails look like the kind of broomsticks witches fly around on." And so it went.

Adelheid was the prettiest of the four of us. She had big blue eyes and a long braid of golden blond hair that fell from the back of her head. Gerda drew the best pictures. I tried in vain to copy them. My little fingers were still too clumsy. I did my best to make colorful flowers. They came out looking pretty abstract.

Soon it was dark outside. Strong winds howled around the house, while the tree branches scratched against our large Berlin window—a kind of early picture window. It really felt spooky. The special donuts were long gone, so Adelheid made chocolate milk and buttered slices of bread for us. While munching away, I happened to look at the window and couldn't believe my eyes. A horrible ghost-like creature with a huge orange head, flickering eyes, and a hideous toothless grin appeared to rise up from below.

Dropping my bread and cup, which spilled brown

milk all over the table, I threw myself underneath. With one leg I also managed to kick a nearby side table, thereby causing a big, valuable vase to fall to the floor and break into hundreds of pieces. I was shaking all over. Why were the others laughing so hysterically? "Stop this nonsense immediately, boys!" Waltraud screamed as she banged against the window. She knew the monster was the handiwork of her twin brothers. "You're just jealous because you missed out on Frau Zimmermann's donuts. Go home right now and behave yourselves!"

Leaving my hiding place and seeing the broken china, I started crying. "Look at what you've done, Lorchen!" Gerda yelled. "It was Mutti's favorite Rosenthal vase from the Hanks." This remark hardly consoled me. So I sought refuge in Adelheid's arms while the others picked up the pieces.

This was not meant to be the final shock of the evening, however. In North America October 31st, All Hallows' Eve, is celebrated as Hallowe'en, a festival having its roots far back in Druidic rites to drive away the evil spirits. In all my subsequent years of living in Western Germany, I never saw anything like it. There must have been a remnant of Celts living near the Baltic Sea, with the result that this custom survived in East Prussia up to those pre-War days. Nearly thirty years later, a week after my arrival in the United States, I was surprised once more when, on October 31st, ghost-like figures let themselves into our unlocked living room in New Haven and demanded "Trick or treat!" Then I remembered that long-ago night of my childhood in a land that no longer existed.*

Going back to that particular night in Kaltenborn, I

---

* In the meantime, the full American version of Hallowe'en, like so many other American customs, has taken root in Germany, to the joy of merchants throughout the land.

remember that it was well past our bedtime, 10 p.m. We were rubbing our eyes, and Adelheid Napierski was about to send her sister over to tell the parents that the girls needed to stay a little longer, when a large car with a Red Cross emblem pulled up to our front door. Loud knocks followed. When Adelheid opened it, we saw past her to our parents, with bandages on their heads, arms, and legs, being led in by two nurses. They entered the living room, sat down, and explained what had happened.

"After dinner with our friends," Pappa recounted, "we noticed the fog had thickened, and our driver decided we should leave immediately. Once on our way, it got so bad that the car's headlights could hardly penetrate the gray mass in front of us. And then it happened. The car jerked to one side, glass flew, and we landed in a ditch next to the stream. Managing to crawl out of the badly damaged vehicle, Mutti and I noticed we were covered with blood. We called to the driver, who followed our voices and found us. He appeared unharmed. 'Stay here,' he said, 'while I go to the next police station to get help.' So we sat on the damp ground for what seemed an eternity. We were shivering from both the shock and the cold. Finally, the driver returned with the police, who took us to the Red Cross station, where they determined that we had only minor surface wounds, which they wrapped in these bandages. Don't worry, children!" Pappa concluded. "It looks worse than it is. We should be all healed and back to normal before you know it."

Our tears stopped, though our hearts continued to pound. We sighed with relief, our friends went home, and we fell exhausted into our beds. It was a night I would remember for a long time—Hallowe'en 1935 in Kaltenborn, East Prussia.

16

Christmas, 1935

The first snowflakes were falling. I was sitting in front of the big window, my nose glued to the glass. Small as I was, I knew Christmas couldn't be far away.

It now got dark in the middle of the afternoon. Mutti was busy baking all kinds of cookies. She let Gerda and me help decorate them with frosting and tiny colored candy pearls. Together with Pappa, she even made marzipan, an elaborate procedure requiring that soaked almonds be passed through a special grinder, then mixed with diluted powdered sugar and a few drops of rose water. After the dough was rolled out on the table and pieces in different shapes were cut out, Pappa would treat them with red-hot pliers to give them brown burn marks as decoration. Finally, the finished products would be placed in tin boxes so that the flavor could settle in. All this was done in imitation of the famous Koenigsberg Marzipan, which is manufactured to this day in Bavaria, Southern Germany, by descendants of the original East Prussian family from Koenigsberg.

Time seemed to pass more slowly during the months leading up to Christmas, due no doubt to our impatience. Gerda's friend Adelheid spent many evenings with us, and the two older girls would take turns reading fairy tales out loud. In between, we memorized and practiced speaking our Christmas poems, which we would be asked to recite on Christmas Eve to please our parents and Santa Claus. Four weeks before the Holiday, the door to Pappa's private office, the *Herrenzimmer*, was closed and locked, not to be opened till the evening of December 24th. We tried to peek through the keyhole, but it was sealed on the other side. Nothing had been left to chance. We knew that the big evergreen tree would soon be in place, but we would not see it until the Holy Night when it would be aglow with lit candles.

Finally the big day arrived. It was still early afternoon. Outside the fresh-fallen snow glittered under the winter sun. Mutti had filled a big basket with packages. In order to help the time pass faster for us, she told us to get out our sled. Placing the basket and me on top, she told Gerda which parcels to drop off at the Napierskis and which to take to other families in the village. The sled glided easily over the pulverized snow. Surprised, Frau Napierski accepted the packages with a grateful smile. We knew they were filled with apples, cookies, and other sweets. "We'll open them tonight under the tree," she said, as one of her smaller boys tried to snatch a package away from her. The other children, standing behind her, were eager to come along with us. Throwing on their coats and knitted hoods, they ran outside, and off we all dashed to our next destination. One by one, we placed the parcels in front of the appropriate doors.

Soon our work was done. It being still early, the boys suggested a little extra excursion into the woods. Perhaps we could see some animals playing in the snow. We didn't hesitate, and before long our little party was surrounded by a winter wonderland. The slanting rays of the afternoon sun made everything sparkle like diamonds. The snow dust kicked up by our sled, meanwhile, floated in the air like tiny points of light.

Hush! What was that? A tall pine tree had just

released a pile of snow from its branches. The effect was that of a silvery veil extending itself in mid-air, or was it the wing of an angel gliding through an enchanted forest? One of our Christmas stories told about how on Christmas Eve bands of angels would roam around in the sky. I wondered.

"Horst, do you know where we are going?" Gerda suddenly asked, a trace of concern in her voice. "I am sure we've passed this same spot a little while ago." We all looked around.

"This must be the right direction," Horst replied. On we went. The sunlight suddenly disappeared, leaving purple-blue shadows on the snow-covered ground. It was icy cold. I clapped my hands and felt how frost had begun to bite my toes. "I want to go home," I yelled and began to cry. I was afraid we would get lost in the now-dark forest.

"Did you hear that?" Gerda shouted. "Listen! Did you hear those bells?"

"O Ja!" I said, hope returning. "Maybe it is Santa Claus with his sled," I thought. Then sure enough, a horse and sled appeared with a bearded man on top. It wasn't Santa, though—only old Herr Pukrop. Whenever he passed through the village, he would always let Gerda take the reins and guide the wagon. She was as fond of horses as Mutti.

"Herr Pukrop!" She ran up to the wagon. "We seem to be lost here. Everything looks the same in the snow. Can you please guide us home?"

He nodded and motioned for Gerda to climb up and sit down next to him. We should have known better than to have trusted those Napierski boys, I thought. They always got us into trouble.

It was pitch dark by the time we arrived at the school house, although it was only 5:30 in the evening. We were just in time for the traditional Christmas Eve dinner—hot dogs, mashed potatoes, and sauerkraut. We were famished from our adventure and couldn't wait to start eating.

"Where were you?" Pappa wanted to know. "What took you so long to deliver a few presents and come home?" Between mouthfuls, we told him our story. "Thank God for old Herr Pukrop!" Mutti sighed. "Now hurry up and change into your Christmas dresses! When I ring the bell, the door to the Christmas room will be opened, and you can go in."

Soon enough all this happened. Soft light flooded out through the wide-open doorway. On entering, we saw the magnificent tree in all its glory, lights flickering and ornaments glittering. What a breathtaking sight! Oh, and underneath were all the gifts we had awaited for such a long time. (In those days it was not the custom to wrap presents in special paper; they were placed under the tree just as they were. That was one of the reasons for keeping the Christmas room under lock and key until the right moment.) Naturally, I felt the urge to reach for my presents right away, but no. Gerda was nudging me. "Lorchen, not yet! First we have to recite our poems."

In the middle of my performance, I gasped in disbelief. Could it really be? There next to the tree was a big doll's house. Moving closer, I found it had two rooms upstairs and two downstairs. Not only that, but all the rooms were fully furnished with miniature furniture, lights, curtains, pictures, everything. This turned out to be a surprise gift for us both from Oma Lina and Opa Ernst. The latter had spent the better part of the year painstakingly building the house and creating all its contents. Overjoyed, we ran to our parents and hugged them.

"Now children, be quiet for a moment," Mutti said. "You'll have the whole evening to play." Pappa then took a big book from the shelf and, sitting in his large armchair, read us a story about the birth of Jesus. Then Mutti began to sing "Stille Nacht" ("Silent Night"), with the rest of us joining in. Other songs followed. Finally we were allowed to return to our toys. We became so involved in our play, in fact, that we nearly forgot to feast on our *bunte Teller*—plates for each family member containing Christmas candies, cookies, chocolates, nuts, apples, oranges, and our home-made marzipan. Because of this tradition, Christmas Eve supper was always a light meal in East Prussia.

Despite the late night, Gerda and I were up early so we could hurry back to our new toys. It was a beautiful, sunny Christmas morning. So, after breakfast we put on our snowsuits and ran outside. Flopping down on our backs in the soft, fluffy whiteness, we moved our arms up and down to make snow angels. I seemed to be bursting with happiness. As I lay on my back, I looked right up into the sun. Closing my eyes immediately, I saw dark purple circles for a while. Oh, God! What had I done? No one had ever told me how dangerous it was to stare into the sun—that doing this could make you go blind. It took a little time for my vision to return to normal. Fortunately, it did. With wet patches of snow all over our snowsuits, we ran back into the house. Christmas had finally come!

17

New Year's Eve, 1935

O n Sylvester (New Year's Eve) we children were allowed to stay up till just past midnight. Herr Engelhardt, the forester, and Herr Leidereither, the village policeman, and their wives arrived—each man with a bottle under his arm—to help our parents celebrate the end of the old year and the beginning of the new. Their kids came too. In the early evening our battery-powered radio filled the house with the happy sounds of *Die Fledermaus*. Each year Strauss's operetta was broadcast live direct from Vienna. As I learned later, this was already an established tradition that has been continued up to the present. The only difference is that nowadays people all over the world can see as well as hear the transmission in high-definition color TV via satellite.

We children, sitting around the dining-room table, could hear the lovely music from the other room. With us were our three guests. First there was Helga Leidereither. With her brown eyes and short, black hair cut in front in bangs, she was the youngest in her family. Her two big sisters were old enough to have been invited to the New Year's Eve dance at the *Arbeitsdienst* Camp. Next to Helga sat the brother and sister Werner and Anneliese Engelhardt. Both had blond hair, with Anneliese's done up into nice pigtails. The children were Gerda's age or a little older. As usual, I was the baby.

We were playing a game called "Eat the Chocolate"

that children often played back then at birthday parties and other celebrations. Chocolate bars left over from Christmas would be wrapped in paper and secured with a piece of string tied in a bowknot. A single die was passed around until someone rolled the number six. Then, while the next person was trying for a six, the first player had to use the knife and fork to untie and unwrap the chocolate bar. If the second person was unlucky, the first might even get to cut off and eat a piece or two of chocolate. This had to be done with knife and fork also. The moment player #2 threw a six, however, player #1 had to pass the chocolate and cutlery on immediately. Number 2 then got to cut and eat to his heart's content until #3 hit a six. Later players usually had a least one piece and often more. So, as the smallest child playing, I was always happy when I did not have to go first.

Naturally, we each tried to throw the die faster and faster, since it was a special thrill to snatch the fork away before the last player had a chance to put the candy into her mouth—a situation that always caused loud fits of laughter. Eventually, everyone got more than their fill of chocolate, since there was always a good supply of bars on hand. Later on, of course, our tummies generally didn't feel so good.

When the big clock struck midnight, we joined the adults in the other room. We all said *"Prosit Neujahr!"* ("May all be well in the New Year!")—the adults toasting with champagne and we kids with fruit juice. Then, with lit sparklers, adults and children alike ran out into the cold night and wished the same to Mother Nature and all her creatures.

It was really quite late now for us kids. Despite our long afternoon naps, we were ready for bed and slept peacefully into the New Year.

18

Angry Words

I t was now 1936. Ahead lay another long winter, with icy winds, snow, slush, and more snow. Gerda and I got sick in turns. No wonder, given that our house was part of the school building. We were exposed to all kinds of germs the children brought with them—measles, mumps, even yellow jaundice. I also suffered from periodic ear infections, which were particularly painful.

To lighten up those long, gray months, Pappa arranged for movies to be sent down from our provincial capital, Koenigsberg. Emil Rabe, boss of the *Arbeitsdienst* camp, provided the necessary equipment, and Herr Naht's ballroom, our erstwhile opera house, now became the village movie theater. Every Saturday night there would be a full house. For most of the villagers, who had neither the time nor the money to take the daily mail bus to Neidenburg, this was their only opportunity to take in a show. For me it was my first encounter with the movies. Mostly I fell asleep in the darkened room with the flickering pictures. It was my bedtime anyway.

On the walk home, Pappa had to carry me because I was afraid of the dark shadows cast on the pavement by the moonlight through the tall trees. To me the street seemed full of deep, dark trenches. I had doubtless become afraid of the dark in recent months from hearing too many stories about the ghosts of soldiers who would come out at midnight to continue their battles. To cure me, Mutti tried sending me down to the dark cellar all alone to bring up some potatoes or carrots. Crying did me no good. "Go ahead," she commanded. "There are no such things as ghosts," she insisted in a firm voice.

I walked downstairs as slowly as I could, singing loudly to give myself courage. This seemed to work until one day, as I was grabbing for a potato, I got something else instead—something cold and slimy that jumped out of my hand. I screamed. A toad with bulging eyes looked back at me. I dropped everything and ran upstairs as fast as I could. "Mutti!" I screamed. "There are toads in the cellar, and they are just as bad as ghosts! I'm not going down there any more, and I mean it! Next time you can send Gerda!"

As the winter progressed, the normally serene mood in the house seemed to change. I remember nights when we were awakened by loud voices from below followed by Mutti crying. Once Gerda and I snuck downstairs and looked through the kitchen door, which was ajar. We could make out Pappa walking back and forth, in a heated discussion with Mutti. She was leaning against the table. We heard more than we could see.

"Don't waste your time, Hans, drinking with those men. They are not your friends. More likely than not, they are waiting for you to say something against the government so they can have something on you. Don't forget what happened in Worplack, when Frankenfeld and his Nazi friends called you a Communist because you showed concern for the underpaid farmhands. Once they found out that you did not vote for Hitler, they got you dismissed as principal of the school!"

"I know, Trude; I know," Pappa replied. "But no one here or any place else will ever convince me that Hitler is Germany's savior. Not even Emil Rabe, who is basically a good person, but when it comes to *der Fuehrer*, he is as blind as the others. Fortunately, he respects me for who I am. I know he will never harm me."

"Ach, Hans," Mutti persisted, "if you had only taken the advice of your teacher friends back in the early Thirties when they were asking for German teachers in Uruguay, we would not be in the mess we are today." Raising her voice, she added, "But no. You had to listen to your mother, who shamed you into staying here by saying that you would be deserting her, a widow."

"Leave my mother out of this!" Pappa shouted. Then, reaching for the dish rack, he started throwing the saucers to the ground one by one.

Gerda and I had had enough. Shaking, we half-climbed-half-stumbled upstairs to our beds, where we cried ourselves to sleep.

19

Pappa and I Go to School

The year 1937 would prove very eventful for our family, with lots of changes for us all. As village schoolmaster Pappa always went to school. But as 1937 began, he was called up for "routine" army training, as his draft notice put it. Now he too would be a student and have to go to another kind of school. Some weeks later he returned home several pounds lighter.

After my sixth birthday on March 4th, it was my turn. Unlike America, where children start school in the late-summer or early fall, in the East Prussia of the Thirties, the school year began like Nature's year in the spring. Consequently, I started school right after Easter.

When Mutti began combing and braiding my hair on that first school day, I held tight to my big cone-shaped paper container filled with candy. (This tradition of sending children off to their first day of school with such "candy cones" is still common in Germany today.) My first-day cone notwithstanding, I doubtless joined thousands of my peers and began to cry.

"This is a happy day, my child. Why are you crying?" Mutti asked, wiping away my tears.

"I am afraid," I answered, still sobbing, "because I can't read and write like the other children, and when they don't know their lessons, Pappa scolds them."

"You little *Dummkopf* [silly]!" Mutti laughed.

71

"This is only your first day. Starting today you'll learn little by little what you need to know. Pappa doesn't expect you to know things before you start school!"

The bell was ringing. Relieved, I rushed into the classroom. There was Pappa, sitting in front of us and smiling. He asked us newcomers easy questions, told stories, and showed us the ABCs on the blackboard. Before I knew it, the morning was over, and I was free to enjoy my candies.

20

A Nazi Rally in Neidenburg

After Easter, Gerda left home for Neidenburg. There she stayed with our great grandparents so that she could attend middle school. (Pappa's village school was only a *Volksschule*, or elementary school.) Before leaving, she received a new two-piece dress complete with a matching cap crocheted in shimmering silk threads by Oma Lina. When she put them on, she looked like a little lady and almost grown up to me. Pappa took a picture of her in this outfit on the steps leading to our front door. Later in Neidenburg, he bought her a bicycle so that she could visit us on weekends in case she got homesick. For a while, though, she enjoyed being the only child in Tante Frieda's household.

When summer vacation came, so did our playmates from the city, Lotte and Dorle Hank. As before, we enjoyed spending time with them at our lake with the private sand beach in the middle of the forest.

One day some exciting news came through our radio—the Olympic Games in our nation's capital, Berlin, were about to start. As we sat around the receiver in the corner, the older girls tried to explain to me what the Olympic Games were. A week later a colorful postcard arrived from Berlin. Sent by Opa and Oma Radtke, it showed all the flags of the nations which were competing in Berlin. Mutti explained that Opa and Oma were there visiting with Opa's younger sister, Else, and had been lucky enough to get some tickets for the Games. Later, we received a large black-and-white photo showing them standing in front of the *Reichssportpalast*, the Imperial German Sports Stadium, which served as the main venue of the Games. In their elegant clothes they looked like very important people to me even if they were only Opa and Oma.

A week after the Olympics, Pappa's empty classrooms were filled with new commotion. Women clad in white with red crosses on their matching caps were going in and out carrying packages and boxes. Mutti together with Frau Engelhardt, Frau Leidereither, and other women from the village had enrolled in a course, organized by Deaconess Luise, to become certified Red Cross Volunteers.

All this activity was naturally very exciting for us kids. If we kept quiet, Mutti informed us, we could stay in the corner and watch some of the demonstrations. We could even volunteer to play "victims." Soon enough we emerged wearing bandages around our heads, hands, arms, and legs. When Mutti graduated from this program, she received a pin with the Red Cross symbol on it. From then on, she always wore her pin with pride on her overcoat. Little did she realize that one day that pin and the knowledge it represented would help save our lives. But all that would come later.

In the beginning of June, Emil Rabe showed up at our house. He was a tall, stocky man, bald, with a friendly smile. He had come to tell Pappa that he and his classes would be required to take part in a rally in Neidenburg that the *Arbeitsdienst* and Hitler Youth were holding for the East Prussian *Gauleiter* [Governor], Erich Koch. The latter was scheduled to give a propaganda speech which all good Germans in the area needed to hear. In obedience to a law recently enacted in Berlin, every boy and girl over ten in the village had already been enrolled in the Hitler Youth. They were to show up in their appropriate outfits. Herr Rabe added that he would provide enough trucks to transport all the youth, while our family could ride with him in his big car.

When the big day arrived, we went. It was a good opportunity, we rationalized, to visit our great grandparents, our two aunts, and Gerda. By the time we arrived at the large square in front of city hall, the *Arbeitsdienst* boys were already lined up and standing at attention. Before long, Neidenburg's Hitler Youth groups marched in from a side street. They were carrying lots of flags which waved slightly in the cool morning breeze. All the flags were red, with white circles in the middle containing a crooked black cross. I had never seen so many flags before.

Great excitement seemed to fill the air. A band added to it by playing march music. Since only a few parents in our village could afford to buy their children official uniforms, the majority came in everyday clothes. The actual uniforms for girls consisted of black skirts, white blouses, and a black scarf held together in front with a brown leather clasp. The boys meanwhile wore black pants, beige shirts, and black scarves likewise held together in front with a twist of leather. On their left arm they wore a red-cloth band with the new German flag on it.

Pappa was told to line the school children up along one side of the square, with me among them. Now we waited for this important person named Erich Koch. And we waited a long time. Soon, we children were entertaining ourselves by making up silly rhymes involving the Gauleiter's name. (*Koch* in German means "cook.") It was a mild June day. The morning sun, shining brighter now, accented the colorful scene. Who would not be impressed by all this?

Finally the moment we had been waiting for arrived. Cheers arose from all sides as a large column of S.A. (Storm Troopers) marched in. They were led by a medium-sized man who lifted his arm repeatedly and gave the crowd the new German salute. With his size, little mustache, and yellow uniform, he looked to me like a double of Hitler, whom I had seen only in newspaper pictures.

I listened to the words of the song the troops were signing. "It's the 'Horst Wessel Song,'" the boy next to me whispered. "Raise the flag! The S.A. is marching in with its solemn, steadfast steps!"

"Who is Horst Wessel?" I wanted to know.

"He is the person who wrote the song," the boy explained, "but was shot during one of the rallies in Berlin. Now he is one of our heroes."

Suddenly, the S.A. column came to a halt. Erich Koch, accompanied by two adjutants, walked smartly along the rows of the Hitler Youth and *Arbeitsdienst*. In response to his salutes, given with a broad smile, a hundred throats yelled back, *"Sieg Heil! Sieg Heil!"* The city square echoed their enthusiasm.

While these things were going on, I noticed that Mutti was quietly talking with the woman next to her. I then turned around and saw Pappa's stern face. He didn't seem a bit enchanted by all this spectacle.

Soon it was over. Koch and his party had disappeared into city hall. We children were relieved that we were now free to walk away. I should add that this was the first and only Nazi rally we ever watched in person as a family. Of course we saw lots of others in the newsreels at the movies.

As for Erich Koch, the man who that morning had presented us with the image of a caring father of his province, he would be responsible in January 1945 for the terrible suffering of millions of its civilian citizens—mostly women and children, the old and the sick. Believing fanatically like most of his comrades in Germany's *Endsieg,* or Final Victory, he refused to give an order for evacuation until it was too late for most people. By then, the marauding, vengeful Red Army came sweeping through our land. The last-minute refugees froze to death as they fled down icy, wind-blown roads; drowned in the Baltic Sea; or were raped and massacred by the victorious soldiers from the East.

21

Deaconess Luise Saves My Life

The following summer we again had many visitors. Among those I remember were Tante Frieda and my godmother Grete Baatz, Mutti's best friend, with her platinum-blond two-year-old son Harry from Neidenburg.

It was fun playing with him. He had curls every girl could envy. As for Tante Grete, I was particularly fond of her. She was always elegantly dressed. Not only that, but she made the most beautiful dresses for Mutti. What fascinated me the most, though, was the way she talked. Mutti called it a lisp. Soon I began imitating her and developed one of my own. Years later, when I was a teenager, it took private lessons from an actress to rid me of my lisp.

Over the past two years, Pappa, with the help of some boys, had worked diligently to cultivate our backyard. Beginning with the same sandy soil you could see in the bottom of the nearby lakes, he composted the land. Now everything grew in abundance. Mutti even had her beloved asparagus beds. Our summer meals consisted mainly of a variety of vegetables and fish, the latter delivered fresh to the house each week by Herr Sublattni, the fisherman. I like fried fish well enough but absolutely detested the creamy fish soup Mutti cooked far too often. Of course, we were not allowed to leave the table until we had cleaned our bowls. Oh *weh!* Sometime I sat there for an hour.

The years of hunger after World War One had made Mutti especially strict in this regard. "Eat whatever God provides," she would say. "You never know what the future will bring. One day you may long for a bowl of soup like this." Unfortunately, not too many years later, her words proved all too true.

In those days I seemed to get stomach cramps quite often. One day it was so bad that I ran a high fever and could not keep even water down. Mutti sent Gerda for Deaconess Luise. At that time country villages like ours did not have a doctor, so usually one of the women known for her expertise in such things would be called upon. On arriving, Deaconess Luise found me curled up in a fetal position. "Get me a bucket of cold water. Be quick," she shouted. When Pappa returned with it, she threw the entire contents on me. I awoke from my "blackout" to hear her say, "The child needs an enema."

"When did you last go to the bathroom?" She asked, rearranging her white bonnet. "I don't know," I murmured. "Maybe last week."

"What?" She replied. "How could that be?"

"Well, our outhouse stinks so bad I just couldn't go."

It took a while until my system was cleaned out. Then, exhausted, I fell into a deep, peaceful sleep. The next day I was back to normal. Good Sister Luise had saved my life.

This incident had another positive outcome too. A little wooden chair with a bucket underneath was installed in the corner of the attic closest to Gerda's and my bedroom. That stinky outhouse, now a thing of the past, was my worst childhood memory from Kaltenborn.

22

Uncle Erich's Fiancée

One July morning, as we were eating in the gazebo in the front yard and marveling at the juicy beans climbing up the wall of the barn, we heard a high-pitched ring-ring coming down the road. Soon our gate swung open, and in came Uncle Erich, Pappa's younger brother, balancing on a bicycle.

"Good morning, everyone! I am here to introduce my fiancée, Elly, to you." We looked around, but no one else was there. "Oh, don't worry! She'll arrive tomorrow at noon with the bus. When she's here, I plan to teach her to ride a bike."

The next day he picked her up from the bus station and brought her to us as announced. I was impressed. They made an attractive couple—he with his raven-black hair and green eyes and she, next to him, a blue-eyed strawberry blond. How nice! She even brought me a present, a doll in a sailor suit. She instantly won my heart.

It was a hot day, so after lunch we all went to the lake. It so happened that it was the day for Mutti's lifesaving course. The rest of us went out on the small jetty to watch her in action. I was frightened when she didn't appear for what seemed like a long time after one of her dives. Finally, she came up triumphantly holding a large stone in one hand. She had been required to retrieve it from the bottom of the lake. "Thank God!" I thought.

As I was turning to go back to the beach, someone

pushed me from the side, and I fell into the deep water. "Everyone can swim," I heard a voice yell. Then there was laughter as I struggled to keep my head above water. Suddenly, Mutti grabbed me and put me back onto the pier.

"Do you think that was funny?" I heard Mutti say, addressing one of Herr Naht's sons. I was shaking with sobs. She was not amused. "That was a mean trick to play on a girl who almost drowned when she was two and is just now starting to regain her confidence in the water." I couldn't wait to get home. It made me sad that Gerda had been among the kids who were laughing.

Fresh strawberries and blueberries swimming in milk were the best remedy for my shock. It was a warm summer evening. The songs of the birds and the chirping of locusts filled the air. Sitting together in the gazebo, we listened to Uncle Erich and Tante Elly tell about the latest happenings in their hometown, Allenstein. At that time Uncle Erich was an official in the Allenstein County government. But, as we learned, he would shortly be promoted to a position with the national government in Berlin and would be moving there in October. We were all surprised that he would be leaving Allenstein so soon.

Tante Elly talked about the wedding, set for September. We of course were all invited. I was delighted and proud when she asked me to be her flower girl. Naturally I accepted.

Her bike lesson the next morning was not destined to last too long despite all our cheering. The rough country road proved hardly the best place for a beginner to learn to balance a two-wheeler. After skinning her knee, she gave up. That afternoon we waved goodbye to her at the bus depot. "See you at the wedding!"

The next day at lunch, as I was enjoying my favorite dish, rice pudding with preserved plums, Mutti and Pappa got into an intense discussion. "You see, Hans," Mutti said, "your brother who always lagged far behind you academically is now climbing the ladder of success. It figures. He's been a Party member since 1933."

"True enough," Pappa replied. "Erich is my brother and as an adult entitled to make his own decisions. He'll have to live with them too. As for me, I still believe in merit. The person who laughs last, laughs best."

"My God, Hans, you are still hanging on to those old-fashioned ideas of yours which will not take you anywhere except to another God-forsaken backwoods corner of East Prussia. Wait and see!"

All this sounded strange to me. Hadn't we just enjoyed a nice evening together as a family? What my parents had just said was so hard for me to understand. Mutti sounded scared too. At this point it seemed best for me to go outside and try to forget what I had heard.

(Left) My great-great-great grandmother with Oma Dorchen on her knee, 1869; *(below top)* high school students do required "field work," 1917, caption: "Fatherland, only for you"; *(below bottom)* Kaltenborn, after being burned down by the Cossacks in 1914.

Volks-Abstimmung „Deutscher Tag" Allenstein 1920.
Photo.-Diettrich.

OSTERODE, OSTPR., KGL. LEHRER-SEMINAR

(Above) Mutti *(right)* about to go skating with her older sister, Hanna, 1921; *(opposite top)* East Prussian Plebiscite, Allenstein, 1920; *(opposite middle)* Opa Ernst *(center)* with two colleagues in front of "their" new steam locomotive, Koenigsburg, East Prussia, 1921; *(opposite lower)* Teachers College, Osterode, East Prussia, which became a girls' high school in World War II.

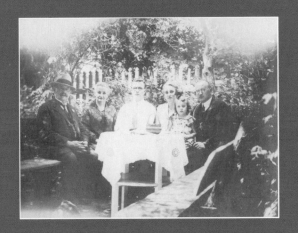

(Above top) Opa Karl, Oma Dorchen, Uncle Erich, Mutti, Gerda, and Vati, Summer, 1930; *(above)* Tante Hanna, Mutti's older (and only) sister; *(opposite top)* Vati's graduating class, Teachers College, 1922 (Vati, the valedictorian, is in the 2nd row, 4th from left); *(opposite middle)* 1,000/1,000,000-Mark note—early inflation after World War I; *(opposite lower)* this billion-Mark note might buy a loaf of bread as the post–World War I inflation deepened.

Vati's and Mutti's engagement pictures, early 1920's

RESZEL

(Opposite top) Me, three months old, 1931; *(opposite middle)* my third birthday—March 4, 1934. I'm between the two "big girls." (Note the cat scratch on my cheek—from the incident described in the book.) *(Opposite lower)* age three, with my favorite hen; *(above)* Crusader Castle, Roessel, East Prussia (now Reszel, Poland)—my birthplace; *(below)* The Worplack Elementary School, July 1933.

(Above top) Waldsee Lake with bath house—
Summer, 1934; *(above)* my great grandparents
celebrate their 60th anniversary. My sister, Gerda,
looks down at me. *(Left)* with big sister, Gerda—
August 27, 1934. "Why did the photographer take
so long?"

(Above) I sit down on Tante Frieda's lap, with Dora Hank on the left and Gerda on the right—Kaltenborn, 1935; *(opposite top-to-lower)* gardening with Tante Frieda—Kaltenborn, 1935; a lake picture in Kaltenborn, 1935—I'm in front; Spring 1936 in Kaltenborn, East Prussia. Vati and Mutti are in the second row, left; sister Gerda is in front of Vati. I'm in the middle (age 5) with the ball. The adults next to my parents are the local forester and his wife.

Official postcard from the 1936 Berlin Olympics

Opa Ernst and Oma Lina in
front of the Imperial Sport
Palace, the main Olympic
venue, Berlin.

23

I Enter First Grade

From the living room and my parents' bedroom, I could see the front of the schoolyard bordered by a fence, which ran along the main road connecting the village with the town. The branches of two linden trees left just enough space between them so I could see the hills on the left side and the meadows in the middle and right. I watched people strolling past and sometimes marching columns of soldiers. Osterode, Mutti told me, was a garrison town, a new word for me.

As an ABC Cadet, as we first-graders were called, I joined Frau Schneehase's class on the ground floor. It was a combined first- and second-grade class. (*Schneehase*, by the way, is the German for "snow bunny," which sounded funny even to us kids.) The time was early September 1937.

Frau Schneehase was a stout, gray-haired, elderly woman with a fleshy face and small, penetrating brown eyes which commanded instantaneous respect. I noticed very soon that she had some pets, while other class members, especially those with Polish-sounding last names, were her black sheep. I myself was content to be in the neutral group.

We first-graders sat in the front two rows. When we looked up, we saw the elevated brown desk of the teacher. Behind it on the wall was a large picture of a man in a yellow-beige jacket. An iron cross hung just below his left pocket. His brown hair was parted on one side and combed over a stern face. His big blue eyes seemed to stare out into the infinite distance.

Of course I knew who it was but wondered why we had not had any Hitler pictures in our schoolhouse in Kaltenborn. Black boards were located on either side of the picture, so it was almost impossible not to glance at it whenever you looked up to copy something from the board.

As first-graders we still had to use little slate boards which could be easily wiped clean when we made a mistake. More often than any other pupil, Frau Schneehase seemed to call on Lisbeth, a blond girl who sat behind me. "Speak Up! Do you have a tongue?" Lisbeth blushed and managed to stutter a few words. "What sort of nonsense is that?" Frau Schneehase asked harshly. "Will you ever learn anything?"

"Ja, Frau Schneehase. I will learn."

"Ach, sit down. You are good for nothing!"

A deep silence lay over the classroom. Not even the boys on the other side of the room stirred. Frau Schneehase sighed. "Children, children, children—what will become of you?" Then turning with a sour smile to another girl who happened to be one of her pets, Frau Schneehase asked her to recite a stanza from a song we had learned the week before. "Very good, my child. Now let's all sing it."

> *Geh aus mein Herz und suche Freud*
> *In dieser schoenen Sommerszeit. . . .*

Go forth, my heart, and look for joy
In the beauty of this summer time. . . .

We were all relieved when the big bell rang indicating recess. Grabbing our snacks, we raced to the school yard, ate, then joined in circle dances where we acted out fairy-tale characters like Sleeping Beauty, the evil Fairy Godmother, and the Prince. Of course, this applied only to us girls. The boys headed behind the school where they prowled around until recess was over.

When I got home after school, we waited until Gerda arrived on her bike from Osterode in order to eat lunch together. One day I cleaned my plate fast because I wanted to play with our doll's house which Mutti had just unpacked. While thus engaged, I could not help overhearing my parents conversing in the background.

"Hans, guess what I heard the other day from Frau Konopka [the janitor's wife]. Apparently your predecessor, Herr Grabowski, was forced to leave when one of the teachers found him kneeling in front of the door of a pretty female teacher who lived upstairs. He was begging her to let him in. After all, he was a married man with two grown daughters. What a spectacle that must have been! Anyway, the school authorities summarily fired them both and asked them to leave immediately. Frau Schneehase, who replaced the female teacher, got here just before we did."

This was a strange story for me. After all, how could a teacher—a grow-up and an authority figure to boot—behave like that? In this way I began to learn more about the world of adults.

"Ach, Emil Rabe must have heard about the Grabowski vacancy," Pappa replied. "He has a friend in the School District office. I'm sure he forwarded my name to them and gave me a good reference based on my work in Kaltenborn. In any case, Trude, it's better for the girls' education that we are here now, still in a small town but close to a city like Osterode. By the way, he says in his letter that he's left the *Arbeitsdienst* and now has a government job in Heilsberg. He also writes that he and Lotte will visit us soon, since she's expecting in a few months."

"Oh, I am so happy for Lotte and can't wait to see her."

Two weeks later they arrived. Lotte Rabe, as I remember, was a tall, slender woman with short, dark hair, big eyes, and very fair skin. Born in the Rhineland, Mutti told me, she had met Herr Rabe through the *Arbeitsdienst.* (Women over 18 were also recruited for this community-works corps.) I loved that she took time before bedtime to read fairy tales to me in her gentle voice. On and off she complained to Mutti about a weakness in her hands and arms. Could this be related to the pregnancy? She wondered. Mutti advised her to see a doctor as soon as she got home. Weeks later we heard that she had been diagnosed with early-stage Multiple Sclerosis. Since my parents had never heard of this disease before, Pappa looked the term up in a medical dictionary. What he read about the progressive stages of MS did not sound hopeful. We all prayed the baby would be born soon and be healthy. I remember crying.

One morning before school started, our bell rang. Opening the front door, Pappa found a stout little girl who offered him a basket full of eggs. "My mother sent them to welcome you, Herr Teacher."

Standing behind Pappa, I was able to get a good look at her. She had a bright smile and big blue eyes. Her blond hair, slicked down with water, was parted on one side, with a thick little curl behind each ear.

"Tell your mother this is very kind of her, but I really cannot accept the eggs without paying for them,"

Pappa answered with a smile. "What's your name, child?"

"Marga Vaginszki" came the answer.

Pappa handed her some money which she accepted with a curtsey. As she turned to go, she looked at me with curiosity. "Marga, you may bring us the same number of eggs each week," Pappa called after her.

After that, Marga and I became fast friends. Although she was a year older, she would often come over to play with me. This friendship has lasted a lifetime. Although we lost track of each other for many years after the War—she and her farmer family stayed behind, part of the remnant of East Prussians, and had to endure the terrors of occupation by the Red Army followed by years of hardship under the new Communist Polish government— we finally reconnected by mail and were re-united at Mutti's burial in 1990 near Munich.

24

Christmas, 1937

December came with sub-zero temperatures. The thought of vacation beginning on December 18 warmed me against the cold, however. Both freedom and Christmas were near. Thank God!

Mid afternoon on the 24th, as dusk was spreading over the landscape, we trudged to the old Evangelical Lutheran Church in town. It was bitter cold. Bundled up, we took shortcuts across vacant fields to avoid frostbite. Nonetheless, we arrived a little late, and the church was already full.

We managed to find seats in the very back. Pappa had to lift me up to see the big tree near the altar. Powerful music came down from above, and everyone began to sing the familiar Christmas anthems. Someone read the story about Jesus' birth; then the old pastor in a tired, broken voice gave the sermon, which I found too long and boring. Mutti whispered that she and Tante Hanna, her sister, had been baptized here. Still, I was not impressed with the old, gloomy building, even dressed up for the Holidays and warmed by flickering lights. For me it was much more special when Pappa read the Christmas story in our cozy Christmas room.

We sang a few more hymns. I was restless to get home. I knew that a hot dinner and drinks were waiting for us. Best of all would be the presents.

The magic of our candle-lit tree was as breath-taking as ever. We recited our Holiday poems, then rushed to the gifts. There were books and games in boxes for two to six people. After Pappa explained the rules to us, we spent most of the even playing them while nibbling on goodies from our *bunten Tellern* [festively decorated plates for each family member that were filled with fruit, nuts, cookies, and Christmas candies]. Oma Lina had sent hand-knitted woolen sweaters and mittens for us kids. They would come in handy during the freezing East Prussian winter days ahead. Oma Dorchen, meanwhile, had given us money to buy fresh fruit and a picture book for me entitled *Little Hans in the Blueberry Wood*. She made sure to note that it had belonged to Pappa when he was my age. I was fascinated to think that my big Pappa had once turned the pages of this very book with little fingers like mine. It was a hardcover book with a colorful illustration on the front and gold lettering. What a special gift for me! I told the other family members.

Mutti and Gerda started laughing as they reminded me of our infamous excursion to gather blueberries back in Kaltenborn. Gerda pointed to the picture of little Hans all dressed up in a blue suit. "His mother sure knew what color suit to dress him in before he went out," Gerda joked.

All in all, it was a fun evening, though not as exciting for me as the year before in Kaltenborn. Still, each Christmas was special in its own way, I thought. Just then the melodious chimes of the wall clock signaled that it was well past our bed time. So we said good night and went off to our room. Tomorrow the bright Holiday would continue.

25

Dancing Hula in East Prussia

During summer vacation, 1938, Pappa allowed us to bring the little *Volksempfaenger* [radio; literally, "people's receiver"] from his classroom into our *Kinderzimmer* [playroom]. One rainy day I invited my friends Annemarie and Marga, whom I had run into at the bakery, to come over after lunch.

"Please turn the radio on to the Koenigsberg station," my older sister, Gerda, said. "They have Fairy Tale Hour with Matthias Wiemann at 2." [Wiemann, a famous stage and screen actor at the time, had a magical voice.] Even Gerda enjoyed listening to him read and found the right station in an instant. First, though, they had another speaker, called Schimkat. The program was called *"Schimkat ist der Ansicht"* ["Schimkat's Opinion"]. He praised all the wonderful achievements of the new German Reich, the glorious times the German people were fortunate to be living in, etc. Happily, the speech was over soon, and we could turn our full attention to Herr Wiemann's tales.

The hour passed much too fast for us, and now it was Gerda's turn to listen to her favorite program. As she slowly scanned the dial, she hit on some lovely guitar music with a voice announcing "Hawaii Calls"—then in German, *Hawaii Ruft.* The announcer continued in German: "This is our weekly program from the beach at Waikiki. The musicians and singers are standing under the big banyan tree in the courtyard of the historic Moana Hotel, the oldest hotel in Waikiki. In the background, the mighty Pacific Ocean is licking the shore with waves glittering in the moonlight. Can you hear the roar?" The music had stopped for a moment. We listened in awe. None of us had ever even been near the seashore. When the music started again, lovely male and female voices sang melodies in a language we did not understand. "That's English," said Gerda knowingly. She was studying it in school.

The announcer painted the scene for us: "While you are listening to this Hawaiian music, three women clad in colorful gowns with floral designs begin to dance in front of the musicians. They move their arms and delicate hands gently up and down in a kind of sign language that acts out the meaning of the words. Meanwhile, the movement of their feet and knees make their hips sway back and forth to the music. Their dance is called The Hula. The beautiful long hair of the women is adorned with big blossoms worn on one side of their head. The fragrance of their flower garlands, or leis, fills the air all around us."

Spellbound, we begin to move around the room in time to the music. We do our best to follow the "instructions" we had just heard. We feel transported into a fairyland far beyond our familiar East Prussian village. When the program is over, we hum the strains of "Aloha `Oe," while plucking our noses in an attempt to produce something like the sound of the steel guitar. We laugh hysterically as we realize we have invented something new— a nose guitar.

"Do you know where Hawaii is?" Gerda asks with a superior grin. "Oh, it must be next to a large ocean far, far away," we all yell at once. "Yes, even farther than the moon," Marga adds. "Hawaii is a group of islands in the middle of the Pacific Ocean, beyond Europe and even North America," Gerda explains with a smile filled with the pride of knowledge. "You're right. It is very far away. Isn't it fantastic that we can be connected in an instant with sounds from the other side of the world?"

It was one of those moments when future events cast their shadow on the present. I recalled this scene from my childhood when in 1968, a few months after moving with my family to Honolulu, I stood on the very spot from which that Hawaii Calls show had been broadcast to East Prussia in 1938. I also had the privilege to be in the audience for the last performance of the Banyan Court musicians just before we left the Islands in 1972. I was moved to tears not only because of our imminent departure but also because of the precious memory from a childhood and a homeland long gone. *Aloha 'Oe* . . . until we meet again.

26

Oma and Opa Visit the Reich

The following Saturday Opa Ernst and Oma Lina visited us. They had just returned from a two-week vacation to southern Germany and wanted to stop first in Osterode before returning home. Oma emptied a large shopping bag filled with red and green grapes she had bought in Nuremberg. We were overjoyed. Grapes were less expensive there, closer to where they were harvested, than in the far-northern reaches of East Prussia, she informed us.

After they had freshened up, we all sat around the coffee table, eager to listen to their adventures. In Munich they had visited many of the historic sites and art galleries. Opa added with a broad smile that they had also gone to the Hofbraeuhaus. That was fun for him, since, though he was not a drinker—his profession prohibited alcohol on the job--, he enjoyed a good glass of beer on his days off. "Ja," he allowed, "the draft beer in the Hofbraeuhaus was very good indeed!"

"The Bavarian countryside is so beautiful with its spotless villages and farmhouses with flower-adorned balconies!" Oma exclaimed. "And the castles King Ludwig II built are unbelievable—they seem to have jumped right off the pages of a fairytale book.

"After returning to Munich we had one day left

94

before we were scheduled to travel north. So we decided to take a little streetcar trip to a village located on the banks of the Isar River, a place called Gruenwald. It was such a clear day that while sitting on the terrace of the Castle Hotel [Schlosshotel] we could see beyond the lush Isar Valley to Germany's highest mountain, the Zugspitze, on the horizon. What a beautiful, serene place Gruenwald was!"

How could Oma ever imagine that she and Opa Ernst would end up spending their last days, just after World War II, in this very village!

"Our next stop," Oma continued, "was Nuremberg, where we planned a visit of two-and-a-half days—just enough time to explore the medieval part of this historic city. When we arrived, however, there was a lot of commotion at the railroad station, with throngs of people including Hitler Youth and men in S.A. uniforms getting off their special trains.

"We fought our way to the exit, but when we entered the street, the scene was similar. Truck loads of uniformed people were driving through the city, seemingly to the same destination. Not surprisingly, it was hard to find a hotel room. We finally settled on a private pension, breakfast included, on the outskirts of town. After all the traveling, we decided to take the rest of the day off and go to bed early. The next morning we were awakened by loud marching music from the streets. When we looked out the window, we saw that all the houses across the street had been decked out with red swastika flags. 'What's going on?' We asked our landlady. Raising her eyebrows in surprise and disbelief, she replied with a sardonic smile, 'Is it possible? Don't you know that the Party's Annual Rally is taking place here today?'

"'No, we had no idea. We're from East Prussia and are only vacationing here,' we replied.

"'Oh, East Prussia,' she laughed. 'Isn't that where the fox and the hare say goodnight to each other, as the saying goes? All the more reason, my dears, why you need to attend this event! By the way, I have arranged for a bus to take my guests to the rally grounds. Would you like to go along?'

"We looked at each other and nodded. There was no hope of getting to the Old City anyway, given the likely traffic, and all the museums and shops would be closed.

"Since we arrived early, we were able to choose seats in the 5th row near an exit. It was unbelievable how many people, mostly in uniforms, streamed into the stadium. Soon it was filled to capacity. Squad after squad of S.A. troops and Hitler Youth, male and female, holding stiff swastika banners like shields in front of them, marched smartly into the middle of the field. March music filled the air. All around the stadium long swastika banners were hanging from tall masts. With all this commotion, it was hard to talk to each other.

"Ernst turned to his neighbor and asked what would happen next and when the program would begin. 'It starts when the Fuehrer arrives,' he said, giving us a strange look. 'Don't you know that ever since that criminal planted a bomb recently in a hall where he was going to speak, he no longer sticks to a set schedule? We just have to wait until he knows it is safe to arrive.'

"Just then everyone looked up. The sky was cloudless. There was only a single, low-flying airplane, its wings reflecting the golden light of the late-afternoon sun, as it slowly circled the stadium. The crowd went quiet for a few seconds, leaving only the buzzing of the plane's motor to be heard. Suddenly the silence was broken by a thousand throats roaring *'Ein Volk! Ein Reich! Ein Fuehrer!'* [One People! One Nation! One Leader!] in

96

endless-seeming repetition. After that, mixing in, came yells of *'Sieg Heil!'*

"The man sitting next to us jumped up onto his seat and, pointing upward, shouted with great excitement, *'Das ist der Fuehrer, unser Fuehrer!* ['That's the Fuehrer, our Fuehrer!']. Everyone around us was waving with something, even if only little flags, as they repeated the same slogans they heard from below. Some even had tears in their eyes. . . ."

"Oh yes," Pappa interrupted Oma's story. "That man knows how to stir up the masses all right. We've heard some of his speeches on the radio. He and his people are experts in organizing and staging these big public events, but to think they are trying to get the ordinary people to believe that he is coming from above like their savior is really too much!"

"I wonder whether it was really Hitler's plane and not just a commercial one taking some bird's eye pictures," Mutti asked.

"Yes, you might be right, Trude," Oma replied, taking the floor again. "We could never find out, but what's important is that all these people believed it was the Fuehrer's plane. It's the mystery he radiates. So you heard his speech too, Hans?" Oma wanted to know.

"Yes, a real pep talk to the Volk—the usual nonsense based on his twisted ideology," Pappa replied. "But the crowd ate it up as you could tell from their fervent shouts of approval: *'Fuehrer befiehl, wir folgen Dir!'* ['Fuehrer command us, and we will follow you!']

Ideology was a new word for me, which I could hardly pronounce and which Pappa would have to explain.

Oma nodded sadly, sighed, and continued with her

story. "Twilight had set in by the time Hitler's motorcade arrived. At that moment the stadium spotlights were all turned upward, creating a dome of light over the place. It was really quite a sight, I can tell you! Since we sat near the entrance, we saw him marching by with other officials and uniformed guards, his arm raised straight in the German salute. In a split second, as he turned his head toward us, I caught a glimpse of his big eyes. It seemed as if I had been hit by an icy-blue spark, as if by an invisible force. Oh my, those eyes! I have never seen such eyes.

"By the time I had composed myself, Hitler had already reached the podium, where he was introduced by Rudolf Hess, his Deputy. A new wave of cheers erupted, but as soon as the Fuehrer raised his hand, the silence was immediate. He began with a subdued voice, you know, and talked for a while about how Providence [*die Vorsehung*] had empowered him to unite and lead all German people to a safe and prosperous future. There would be space [*Lebensraum*] and work for all people. That sounded quite good, but the increasingly violent gestures of his arms, hands, and fists belied such good intentions. Soon his sentences were ending in husky screams. I had witnessed that same sort of thing years ago in Allenstein.

"Then I looked at Ernst. Oh God, he seemed as mesmerized as the others around us. I gave him a little poke in the ribs. 'Wake up, Ernst,' I whispered. Then smiling, he turned to me and chuckled.'

"*Ach ja,*" Opa interrupted her. "For a moment he reminded me of Charlie Chaplin," and he laughed.

"Only that he's a little more dangerous," Pappa commented, deep lines forming on his forehead.

"*Ach, Kinder, wir leben in einer sonderbaren Zeit!*

["Children, we live in strange times!"] Oma sighed. "What will become of us? Only God knows!"

Entranced as I was by Oma's report, I was absentmindedly stuffing myself with Mutti's crumb cake [*Streusselkuchen*] until she threw me one of her forbidding looks across the table. That stopped me cold. Picking up some crumbs from my lap, I reflected on what Oma had just said. I tried to reconcile in my mind the imposing picture of the Fuehrer that hung in our classroom with my memory of the funny actor I had seen only once at the movies. What their similarity was I could not figure out. Oh, never mind, I thought.

"On the other hand, Hans," Opa addressed himself to Pappa, "many positive things are happening in our country. The building of the Autobahn [Germany's then-new national highway system, comparable to the Eisenhower Interstate Highway System in the U.S.], for example, has created lots of jobs. There are also those KDF ships," Opa continued.* "When we vacationed last summer on the Baltic, we saw some of them leaving Pillau Harbor. There were crowds of dancing and singing passengers on board. They sailed under the motto, "A free vacation for every hard-working member of the German people [*Volksgenossen*]."

"Yes, I heard about that too," Pappa replied. "There's nothing new under the sun. People in ancient Rome were also kept happy with public gifts of bread and games. But I wonder who will end up shouldering all the costs. Our national treasury must be near bankruptcy as it is."

"What kind of games did people in Rome play?" I wanted to know. All the adults laughed.

---

*KDF = *Kraft Durch Freude*, or "Strength Through Joy"

"Well," Pappa answered, "you'll learn about that later in your history classes. They were pretty bloody games that took place in a big stadium. Trude, is there any more coffee?" Lifting his cup for a refill, he turned to Gerda, who sat glued to her chair and had not uttered a word the whole time. "Have some more cake, *mein Kind*, before it's all gone."

"No thanks," she answered with a dry voice. "I'm not hungry." I wondered what she was thinking.

"Ach, Kinder!" Mutti interrupted. "This Kaffeeklatsch is just too boring for you. Why don't you go to your room and play or read until I call you for dinner?" With that, she motioned us out.

27

The Old Rabbi Tries to Flee

How are you getting along with Rector Pipgorra?" Mutti asked Pappa one day over lunch.

"Well, he is quite different from Tybussek, as you've probably guessed from his appearance," Pappa replied, "but he is smart enough to know his limits."

"What do you mean by that?" Mutti wanted to know.

"Ach, he has problems making up the class schedule what with only four teachers available. So, he's asked me to do it for him. He also wants me to write up his official reports, since his command of German isn't quite what it should be," Pappa said with a faint smile.

"I just can't believe it!" Mutti exclaimed. "And this man is supposed to be your boss!"

"Never mind," Pappa replied, shaking his head. "Since he needs my help, I can keep him at arm's length. He won't bother me. In his rough way he even tries to be jovial. Well, that's how things are. They could be worse. Anyway, the extra work isn't a burden. I can do it all in no time."

"Ach, Hans! I feel bad for you. But you know

best. Nowadays, all a person has to do is become a Party member. Then all the good jobs fall into their lap. That's how it is. It's so unfair."

"Yes," Pappa agreed. "It's too late for opposition now. Anyone inclined to do so will stand by himself. Such a man will only endanger his family, and I don't want to do that to you and the children, Trude."

After listening to this conversation, I went downstairs to my newly found refuge, the big linden tree next to the front gate. On one side it had a strong, nearly horizontal branch, conveniently bare of any smaller branches, just above the wooden fence. Climbing to the top of the latter, I could easily swing myself up to a sitting position. Or if I preferred, I could climb higher to another secure place. From there I could look right into Pappa's *Herrenzimmer* [den] with the antlers on the wall. That was fun! The tree was a natural jungle gym—a good thing too, since in those days schoolyards in East Prussia were not furnished with apparatus for kids to play on.

Now, as I sat there, my head leaning against the trunk, thoughts raced through my mind. Based on what I had just heard, my image of Pip the Strongman lost some of its power. Still, it did not really lessen the fear I felt each morning when he entered our classroom. Why had our life here in Kiefernberg become so complicated? As sheltered as my home life remained, my experience of the outside world gave me more and more reasons to worry.

On Saturday nights there was a lot of commotion in the ballroom next door and the adjoining park. Music, loud singing, laughter, and even very disturbing screams that didn't stop until well after midnight kept us from falling asleep. Whenever my sister and I could find working flashlights, we read books under our down comforters until we finally dropped off.

In the morning we complained to our parents. They said they were annoyed too but that was how the owner of the *Gaststaette* was trying to make a little money, by setting up these ballroom events. There was a huge demand for them on the part of the soldiers stationed near town, and the single girls of the village didn't mind either. Unfortunately, everyone drank too much, and things got out of hand.

"Is that why the women scream so much?" I wanted to know. "Perhaps. Who can say?" Mutti replied, exchanging glances with Pappa. "Well, next time I'll give you some cotton to put in your ears. That way you'll be able to fall asleep more easily," she added.

"Please do!" was my response.

When I talked about all this to my friends, they held their hands over their mouths. Giggling with embarrassment, they tried to tell me what was really going on—something which often took place in barns as well, they said, knowingly. A year or two older than me, they obviously knew a lot more than I did. In this awkward way, I got my first introduction to the facts of life. It all seemed rather strange to me and not all that much fun, either.

On a mild November afternoon, Mutti and I went shopping in Osterode. Suddenly she remembered a promise she had made to Oma Lina to cover Baby Lieschen's grave in the town cemetery with pine branches before the first snowfall. I was surprised that a visible grave was still there after so many years. The cashier at the store agreed to keep our bags for an hour or so while we visited the spot on the crest of a hill overlooking town. On the way, we bought branches from a vendor. Having spread them in no time, we said the Lord's Prayer, I cast one last sorrowful glance at the tiny mound, and we began walking back to reclaim our purchases.

As we walked down the hill, something caused us both to stop short. Leaving a large building in great haste was an elderly man clad all in black. He was wearing a broad-brimmed hat and had a long, white beard. He was carrying two large leather satchels from which some shiny metallic objects were sticking out. They looked to me like candleholders. The man tried to run faster and faster, which must have been hard given how heavy his load was.

"Oh my God!" Mutti exclaimed. "It's the old rabbi. He's still here. Where will he go? There are hardly any secure hiding places for Jews anymore. I hope somebody will smuggle him out of town tonight and help him cross the border into Poland."

Paralyzed and speechless, I followed him with my eyes until he disappeared into a side street. This poor old man was obviously petrified. Why must things like this happen? I wondered.

In silence we continued our walk downhill, picked up our bags, and headed home. Absorbed in thought, Mutti shook her head from time to time but did not utter another word until after we had entered our house.

28

Kristallnacht

The next morning in class, we had to wait quite a while for Pip. Finally he staggered in, dressed in full uniform with shiny medals hanging from his breast pocket. He had a hard time keeping his balance until he reached the tile oven, which he could lean against for support. Then, turning his bloodshot eyes toward us, he attempted to say something. When he opened his mouth, however, he lost control of his upper bridge, which suddenly fell onto his lower lip and changed his face into a frightful mask. Breathing deeply to compose himself, he staggered down a row of benches as he jingled the keys in his pants pocket and exclaimed, "Here comes Santa Claus! Here comes Santa Claus!" No one laughed. When he swung around, his face was gloomy again. He shouted, *"Kinder, kauft Euch Kaemme, es kommt 'ne laus'ge Zeit!"* ["Kids, you'd better buy combs. A lousy time is coming!"] His drunken prophecy proved only too true.

Oh God, how glad I was to get home that noon! When he walked into the kitchen, Pappa was pale. Mutti looked up surprised from the soup she was stirring.

"Trude, have you heard the news?"

"What news?" She asked.

"At 4 this morning a unit of Storm Troopers set fire to the synagogue."

"My God! Now I know why the old rabbi was in such a hurry to leave the building yesterday afternoon as we were returning from Lieschen's grave. Someone must have tipped him off," Mutti said.

"But that's not all," Pappa continued. "I just heard on the radio that in Berlin and other major cities the S.A. and older Hitler Youth have gone on a rampage. They've vandalized Jewish-owned shops and businesses, throwing stones through store windows and painting messages of hate on the walls."

"But why?" Mutti stammered.

"The broadcaster said that the action was in reprisal for the killing of a German diplomat in Paris by a young Jew. I'm sure, Trude, everyone can figure out why he did it, but our propaganda writers have made him out to be the aggressor. Meanwhile, Goering has announced that from now on he plans to take care of the 'Jewish problem' once and for all. He even called the night of rioting *Kristallnacht*, as if it were some sort of celebration."

We ate our meal in silence. Even I felt what a fateful day it had been and was unable to say anything. What, I wondered, would come next?

It must have been a week or two later that very early one morning Mutti went to the farmers' market in Osterode to buy a duck for Sunday dinner. While there, she witnessed an awful scene in the street. Uniformed men with rifles were guarding a truck crammed full of young and old people huddled together in despair. A number of passersby stopped as did Mutti and wondered what was going on. Meanwhile, more people were being brought out of a nearby house by other uniformed men as a second truck pulled up.

Suddenly an elderly man, pushing his way through the crowd, shouted, "Hey, why are you doing this? What have these people done?"

"They are Jews" came the answer. "Are you a Jew lover?" A stocky S.A. guard asked with a strange grimace, as he grabbed the man's collar and pushed him toward one of the trucks. "If that's the case, how would you like to join them?"

"Let me go," the man shouted as he freed himself from the guard's grip. "You have no right to treat me like that! I will report you!"

"Is that so? Be my guest," the guard laughed, with the other soldiers joining in.

Having seen enough, Mutti turned around and walked away in disbelief. Someone next to her whispered, "This was an early call. Usually these brutes show up like cockroaches in the middle of the night when nobody can see them work."

"Do you know what happens to these poor people?" Mutti whispered back.

"Someone told me recently that they are shipped off as undesirables to a work camp in Russia or Poland. These are the latest Government orders, apparently."

"You see, Trude," Pappa explained later when she had returned home, "only one man in that entire crowd showed any civil courage, and he was lucky to get away with it. Who knows? The Gestapo may show up at his door too one of these nights, because in this small town everybody knows everybody. Anyone criticizing the Government is declared a public enemy and put away. This has already happened to the former leaders of the Social Democratic Party. Now no one knows where they are."

For my part, I wished I had not heard such upsetting stories. The walls of our apartment were thin, and when Pappa and Mutti were upset, the volume of their voices naturally increased. Tension in my classroom was more than enough for me to worry about at this time. So, like an ostrich burying its head in the sand, I sought refuge in my books. When I had gone through my private collection, I borrowed from the school library. Most of what was there, to be sure, were heroic tales from the Great War, including stories about Germany's legendary flying Aces. Fortunately, I found a children's book entitled *Antje in Masuren* [Antje in Masovia]. "Antje" is a North German or Dutch girl's name, and Masovia was a region in southern East Prussia, now the Polish lake district. After reading through the first few chapters, which were pleasant enough, I found that it too was a war story. It described the rapid advance of the Russian Cossacks in 1914 as they rode through the Masovian countryside, looting and pillaging everything in their path.

Antje's farm was not spared either. Fortunately, she and her family had escaped into the nearby forest in good time, and their lives were spared. Only after the German Army had taken the area back did they dare return to their village. They found it burned to the ground, their house included. (The same thing had happened to our old village, Kaltenborn, in that war, I remembered.) Antje and her parents were glad to be alive, however, and had hope for a better future.

Somehow this story touched me deeply. Tears came to my eyes. As I finished and closed the book, I was still sitting high up on the stepladder Mutti had recently used to hang the cleaned curtains on the bedroom windows. All of a sudden—I remember the moment clearly—I felt a sense of dark foreboding. I tried to change my mood by jumping off the ladder. Strangely enough, I had developed a recent liking for sitting in high places as if subconsciously to get above the negativity happening all around us. Still, it took a while for that feeling of heaviness to fade away.

The good news was that the apple trees in the Principal's garden, whose blossoms I had admired so much in May, were full of fruit this fall, so much so that we were permitted to pick as much as we liked. The apples were still hard and a bit sour, but we children ate so many of them that soon we all got stomach aches. Mutti also preserved a good many of them for winter. Since we did not have a garden of our own anymore, we had to buy vegetables from the market near our school. I still missed our big garden in Kaltenborn where we children could pluck vegetables fresh from the ground or pick some juicy berries to munch on as the spirit moved us. Yes, everything was different here.

29

Christmas and
New Year's Eve, 1938

Soon it was time again for Christmas preparations. As usual, Mutti acted in a very secretive manner. After supper, she locked herself in the big dining room while we were kept busy doing our Christmas drawings and memorizing our poems. In my mind I imagined a blue-and-white stroller for my doll that I had seen and liked in a toy-store window some time ago. I doubted that my parents could afford it. Still, it was nice to dream about it.

One December morning we heard in class that Christel Rossmann, a quiet blond girl who sat two rows behind me, had suddenly died of diphtheria. It was so hard to believe. I remembered my own struggle with that disease the year before. I had been lucky.

"Mutti, can we celebrate Advent a little today?" I asked her in the afternoon. After sunset she lit two candles on the Advent wreath to indicate the second Sunday before Christmas. Then we sang all the familiar Advent hymns. My favorite was

> *Leise rieselt der Schnee.*
> Quietly the snow is falling.
>
> *Still und starr ruht der See.*
> Still and motionless the lake is resting.

Hoert nur wie lieblich es schallt

Just listen—how lovely it sounds!
Freut euch, Christkind kommt bald.
Be joyful; the Christ Child is coming soon.

Mutti's holiday cookies tasted delicious with the warm milk. Outside night had fallen on the snow-covered earth. Yet here in this room it was cozy by the flickering candlelight. I felt so shielded and protected by love.

Christmas Eve finally came. After the obligatory church visit, I was happy to be back in the warmth of our home. What surprises would be in store for me? I wondered. I became so impatient I could scarcely eat my dinner. Finally the door opened to the *Herrenzimmer.* There the lit tree stood in the corner near the big window—a new wonder for us each year as it filled the room with enchanting splendor.

A single step into the room, and I jumped for joy at what I saw under the tree. Forgetting my poem, I ran to the blue-and-white stroller. There, wearing a new outfit, Ursel, my favorite doll, sat propped up on fancy cushions. I rushed to my parents, whom I embraced and kissed. Having finished her poem already, Gerda pulled me back. With a big smile, I finally recited mine.

My sister was happy with her presents too. She got the well-known Wilhelm Busch Album, with its funny drawings and rhymes. Later in the evening Pappa read to us out of it. She also got a book with horse photographs and several new games.

The Holidays raced by. It was to be our last Christmas in Kiefernberg. Some days later I overheard Mutti talking with Pappa in the kitchen: "You see, Hans, how happy Lorchen was with her special present. It was worth stretching our budget to get it for her, especially when you think how easily she could have slipped away from us last year."

Before we knew it, Saint Sylvester (New Year's Eve) had arrived. This year Professor Altmann and his wife were our guests. Mutti had poached a big carp, which she served with boiled potatoes sprinkled with parsley. The adults toasted with white wine, while we children joined in with our apple juice. For dessert Mutti served canned pineapple slices—a luxury for us—topped with lots of home-made whipped cream. On the table was a little plate with large fish scales. Each of us took one for good luck for the coming year. Strewn about were also little packages containing paper streamers and sparklers, not to be opened, we were told, till midnight.

After dinner Gerda and I excused ourselves and went to our room to listen to a radio program while playing our new games and munching on leftover Christmas goodies. We wanted to stay awake to greet the New Year. After a while we heard piano music from the dining room. Rushing over, we stayed outside the closed door, since we didn't want to disturb the adults. Pappa played the familiar operetta melodies. Soon he began to sing with his full, deep voice. Occasionally the others would join in. When a song ended, everyone laughed.

One of the arias, I knew, he sang especially for Mutti: *"Florenz hat schoene Frauen, die schoenste bist Du!"* (Florence has beautiful women, and the most beautiful is you!") Then came another I knew: *"Sei nicht boese, sei wieder gut."* ("Don't be angry, be nice again.") He always sang her this song after they had had a fight. Gerda and I looked at each other and giggled behind our hands.

When the adults started talking again, the two of us

went back to our room and played some more. When the announcer mentioned it was only a few minutes to midnight, we ran to the dining room. Despite the cold, Mutti had opened a window. At precisely midnight, Pappa shot the champagne cork into the dark night air. Wheeling rapidly, he poured the contents into the glasses Mutti held nearby on a tray. Then we all toasted, kissed, and wished each other a Happy New Year. *"Prosit Neujahr!"* Everyone shouted.

We children lit sparklers and held them out the open window. The adults threw streamers at each other until they were covered from head to toe. Many streamers landed on top of the lamp, where they dangled in their multi-colored glory, adding festivity to the scene. Then someone turned on the radio, and we listened in silence as the bells of the Cologne Cathedral greeted the first day of 1939, a year that would prove so fateful for our family, our country, and the world. In the midst of our merrymaking, however, it seemed like just another well-spent New Year's Eve.

30

The Fuehrer's 50th Birthday and Frau Konopka Gives Birth

t was now April, and the town was preparing for the Fuehrer's 50th birthday. Lots of flags were hanging from windows, and shops displayed large gold-framed pictures of him.

When the big day, April 20th, arrived, uniformed youth from our village gathered in groups in the front schoolyard. I could watch it all from my window, since there were no classes today. Gerda was among them, wearing her new BDM [*Bund Deutscher Maedel*, League of German Young Women] outfit. Radio music blared from the loud speakers until the moment came when the Fuehrer began to address his *Volksgenossen* [Fellow Members of the German People]. After the national anthem was sung, the Hitler Youth at full attention gave enthusiastic voice to the "Horst Wessel Song," their anthem. Then at the end, everyone burst forth with shouts of *Sieg Heil! Sieg Heil!*

Standing in full uniform on the school steps, Pipgorra, with Little Schulz and Frau Schneehase behind him, saluted with a satisfied smile: *"Unserem geliebten Fuehrer, Sieg Heil!"* ["To our beloved Fuehrer, Sieg

Heil!"] The response from the assembled youth came back like an echo. Pappa, standing behind me, watched the whole scene without expression.

Gerda felt comfortable in her **BDM** group, since it gave her the chance to make new friends after leaving high school. It was important for her to be part of her peer group. It's hard to be an outsider at any age, but especially when you're a teen.

A few weeks later there were strange goings-on just below our *Kinderzimmer*, where the Konopka family lived. Hearing Frau Konopka in obvious pain moaning and screaming from time to time, I ran, frightened, into the dining room, where Mutti was sitting.

"Do you know what's going on downstairs, Mutti?" I asked breathless.

"Oh yes, my child. Frau Konopka is giving birth."

"Oh God, is it always that painful?" I wanted to know.

"Labor is hard for all women, but it it's easier for some than for others," Mutti replied. "Frau Konopka isn't that young anymore, so that may be why she's having a harder time. Let's go into Pappa's room now where we can't hear her. Oh and here are some books you might like to look at."

Gerda was already there, sitting at Pappa's big desk, doing her homework. I opened one of the books, then looked up again.

"Mutti, I never noticed her getting bigger like Tante Elly when she was expecting her baby."

"Well, Frau Konopka always wears long, wide dresses. In this case, they were a perfect way for her to

115

hide her growing belly. She told me she did not want people to know she was pregnant, since she already has two grown sons and was a bit embarrassed about the situation. Horst, her oldest, just enlisted in the Army, and Herbert is learning a trade and is in and out a lot. So that should free up space in their apartment for the new baby."

A little later when I was getting some water from the kitchen, I heard another sound from below: the first life-affirming cry of a new human being. Soon Herbert came up to tell us that he had a new baby brother, Helmut.

Herbert was a strong, athletic young man with short, sandy, mane-like hair. Many late afternoons he would practice throwing the discus with a big, round stone. I was amazed at how fast he could whirl around, his arm muscles bulging, before he let loose with his ersatz discus. Mutti leaned out of the window one day and shouted, "Herbert, are you practicing for the next Olympics?"

"Yes, something like that, Frau Zimmermann," he answered and carried on.

31

Northern Lights and Mutti's Dream

About ten days after arriving home from Tante Toni's, school began. It was especially hot that late August, so we spent most afternoons cooling off at the lake. One evening, as I was just about to fall asleep, a strange reddish light coming from the window caused me to open my eyes. I sat up and looked again. No, it wasn't a dream. When I peered out the window, the barn in the distance seemed as if someone had set it ablaze. But I couldn't see any flames.

"Gerdalein," I called in a loud whisper. "Are you asleep already?"

"No, Lorchen. What you are seeing is called the Northern Lights. It sometimes occurs at this time of year when they have the Midnight Sun in the Scandinavian countries. On clear nights some of the rays penetrate our atmosphere and cause a spectacular light show. I've seen it once before when I was living in Neidenburg, but never so red." (She was standing beside me at the window now.) "This is awesome!"

At that moment Mutti entered the room to check on us.

"Oh," she laughed, "I see you already know what it is."

"Yes, Mutti. Look over there," I pointed. "Even our lake is shining like a blood-red mirror. Strange, isn't it?"

Mutti stopped laughing. "Yes. It will fade away soon. You'd better get back to bed. It's late."

The next morning we read in the paper that people could see this celestial light show as far south as Bavaria.

A few days later we had a surprise visit from Berlin—Uncle Erich, Tante Elly, and our new little cousin Brigitte (called Gitti). She was just a year old and very cute. She kept me, the designated babysitter, busy all that day.

There was a sense of unrest in the air. We all felt it. Through our front window we observed countless military trucks moving in both directions along the village road.

"Lots of maneuvers taking place," Uncle Erich noted, with the broad smile of someone in the know.

"I hope that's all it is," Mutti added. "I have never seen so many soldiers in one place."

Vati (pronounced "Fah-tee")—my new, more grown-up name for Pappa—just stared at the floor. He withheld whatever comment he might have made.

One evening as we were all taking a walk to cool off from the heat of the day, I overheard Uncle Erich ask Vati whether he would like to go to Berlin too. He would make sure Vati got a much better position than he could ever find here in the country.

"Thank you, Erich." Vati replied. "But if it means I have to join the Party first, then my answer must be no. You know what I mean."

Uncle Erich shook his head in disbelief. Giving Vati a strange look, he said, "You may regret it one day, Hans."

"We'll just have to wait and see," Vati responded, changing the topic to family matters.

The next morning we took the train to Allenstein to visit our relatives there. In the afternoon when we returned home, we found Frau Konopka sitting on a log in the backyard. She was crying. She held a letter in her hand. Mutti ran downstairs to find out what had happened. Without a word, the woman handed Mutti the piece of paper. When Mutti came back, she told us that Horst Konopka, the eldest son, had died from a sports injury sustained during military training. Unbelievable! How could someone so young die so suddenly? I wondered. He was only 19. In my mind I still saw him coming home from work. He would balance his bicycle with his long legs as he rode through the schoolyard.

"Poor woman!" Mutti exclaimed. "She has lost two sons in such a short time. I'll bring her down some cake. Maybe that will comfort her a little."

One day at lunch time as we were sitting at the table in the *Kinderzimmer*, Mutti recounted the frightening dream she had had that night.

"Hans, in my dream I got up from my bed and walked to the window. It was just before dawn. All of a sudden I noticed some planes circling above the meadows. They were releasing shiny red bombs all over the place. I woke up abruptly and was quite upset. I am so afraid this means a new war."

My spoon dropped into the soup with a splash. I stared at my parents. What I saw is still etched in my memory. Mutti sat across the table from Vati. From my seat I could see their profiles, one to the left, the other to the right. For a moment they looked at each other in silence. Then Vati slowly shook his head and replied, "Oh Trude, you and your dreams! Come on! I just heard on the radio that Stalin has sent a whole train car filled with gold bars to Berlin. Why would he do that if he had any intention of attacking us? I don't think he would be such a fool."

We were all quiet after that. Eventually, my heart slowed down, and we finished our meal.

32

A Fateful Day — 1 September 1939

I woke up from a nightmare and ran to my parents' bedroom door, my heart pounding. I knocked and shouted, "Mutti, may I come into your bed? I'm so frightened!" "Of course, climb in," she responded. "What's wrong, my child?"

"In my dream I saw people running from danger. They were trying to hide in the woods. I was among them, but I could not move." "Oh, that dream was probably caused by your going to sleep on a full stomach. You ate more rice pudding with plums at dinner than you should have," she said. Mutti's explanation calmed me down enough so that I could cuddle up next to her and go back to sleep.

Suddenly I was awakened by terrifying noises. Vati, Mutti, and I jumped out of bed and ran to the window. In the twilight we saw large formations of planes flying overhead in a southeasterly direction. It was so loud I had to cover my ears. Gerda ran into the living room and turned on the radio. The Polish capital, Warsaw, was being bombed by our Luftwaffe. We looked at the clock. It was just past 4 a.m. The announcer went on to say that the German Army had crossed the border into Poland. But why? We would learn the reason later. At the moment, shocked and speechless, we looked from one to the other in disbelief.

We went back to the windows. I jumped up onto the sill to get a better view. Below somebody coughed. I looked down to see a peculiar figure standing in front of the entrance to the school. There, hastily pulling his baggy pants over his white nightgown, with the suspenders still hanging down over his bare feet, was Principal Pipgorra. Seeing us at the window, he pointed to an approaching new formation of planes. "There they go. There they go. Our boys!" He shouted. As he waved wildly with both arms, strands of uncombed hair fell over his eyes and made him look even more grotesque. "What a clown!" I whispered to Gerda. She nodded, but neither one of us felt like laughing.

Another noise now caught our attention—the stamping of hundreds of marching boots. The approaching soldiers were singing, *"Auf der Heide blueht ein kleines Bluemelein, und es heist Erika. . . ."* ["On the heath a little flower blooms, and they call it Erika. . . ."] "Oh my God," I thought, "they are smiling and singing as they march to their death. How I wish this too were a nightmare I could wake up from!"

I wasn't sobbing, but tears were running down my cheeks. I could not stop them. I clearly remember having cried all day with only a few interruptions. I was terrified. I thought of all those military graveyards that surrounded my old village of Kaltenborn. I knew what war was all about.

A group of armed Poles, we heard, had attacked some Germans in the so-called Polish Corridor. For the German Government, that was reason enough to go to war. Everyone in the village was puzzled, and no one knew for sure what had happened. But before long, the propaganda machine, using radio and the newspapers, had successfully done its job.

By mid-September, Poland was overrun by our

troops. I listened to the news every day when I came home for lunch. Frequently there were *"Sondermeldungen,"* special victory bulletins, announced by loud fanfares. Mutti explained that the music was taken from an opera by Richard Wagner. One bulletin I shall never forget. How awesome, I thought, that a battalion of Polish cavalry, mostly officers with drawn swords, would attack a column of German panzers. The announcer laughed. "What a useless suicide mission! Naturally, it did not take long for our troops to overpower them."

Vati had heard this story too. When he came home, he commented, "How heroic those men were! It also shows how unprepared for war Poland was."

It is strange how past events can arise years later, like old, unfinished paintings that need a few more brushstrokes. Fast-forward 50 years to 1989. I was living in Saint Paul, Minnesota, with my family. Mutti, now an invalid, had been staying with us for some years. A colleague of my husband's at the university called one day with an unusual request. His in-laws were visiting from Poland. They spoke no English, but the father-in-law was fluent in German. "Could we possibly stop by your house next Saturday? That will be his 75th birthday, and it would be a special treat for him to be able to carry on a conversation without needing an interpreter."

We were happy to invite them. We were even able to arrange for a cake with "Happy 75th Birthday" written on it in Polish. When the family arrived, Mutti and I greeted them at the front door. Startled, the tall, white-haired gentleman kissed Mutti's hand, then said to me, *"Frau Feldman, Ihre Mutter ist eine Burgfrau!"* ["Mrs. Feldman, your mother belongs in a castle!"] Hearing this spontaneous compliment, Mutti smiled, a little embarrassed but enjoying it all the same. At 83 she was still a stunning woman despite the ravages inflicted by a stroke in 1972.

The scene that followed after we were seated around the dining table touched us all deeply. I brought in the lit birthday cake and placed it in front of our guest of honor. We sang "Happy Birthday" in English, the daughter and the mother in Polish. It was a perfect surprise. He looked down at the inscription, the flickering lights dancing on his handsome face. I noticed big tears streaming down his checks.

He thanked us with shaking hands. Looking at Mutti, I saw that her eyes were overflowing too. He told us a little about his life in Krakow now but also during the occupation in wartime. The German Army had appointed him a traffic officer after it was learned that he was one of the few survivors of that ill-fated cavalry charge back in 1939. Professional soldiers apparently respect such heroic acts, even in the enemy. Mutti and I looked at each other, flabbergasted. We both remembered that story and told him so.

There we were--survivors of a terrible war whom fate had cast as enemies. Yet now, a half century later, we could peacefully share a birthday cake and reflect on how futile war is and how precious life and human relationships are, regardless of where we live. How sad that people mainly gain this wisdom only after great suffering or at an advanced age. Still, we were all grateful to be granted this special moment in time together.

33

Words Can Kill

Sister Gerda stayed busy with hikes and other BDM activities as long as the autumn weather permitted. She also helped Mutti with household chores. Ilse Rex, Gerda's best friend from Osterode, visited us from time to time. She was taking voice lessons in hopes of becoming an opera singer one day, so she would sometimes sing for us in the dining room.

One afternoon Gerda came home looking quite bewildered from a BDM meeting in Osterode. The story which Ilse had related to her and which she now told us was very disturbing.

Apparently a boy from Ilse's neighborhood had had a big fight with his father. It ended when his father yelled, "Is that what they teach you in the Hitler Youth? Shame on you! You're grounded for the coming weekend."

It never came to that because the boy repeated his father's words to the Group Leader of his Hitler Youth brigade. The next day in the middle of the night the Gestapo came and arrested the boy's father. The next morning when the family woke up, they had no idea where their father had been taken—probably to a concentration camp is what we would conclude today.

Devastated, the mother refused to speak to her son from then on. The boy, still in shock from this quick action, was reassured by his Group Leader that he had acted correctly and that it was the responsibility of every good German to turn in any enemy of the Party no matter who it happened to be, a family member or anyone else.

Mutti and I listened horrified.

"Now you see what can happen if you are not careful with what you say outside the house!" Mutti warned. "It is normal for teenagers to have disagreements with their parents. But when they lead to such consequences, that is truly tragic. I feel sorry for that young man. He will have to live with the burden of what he did for the rest of his life."

Gerda nodded, tears in her eyes.

34

Christmas, 1939

Vati got leave to come home for Christmas Eve and the next two days. Mutti decorated the tree as always and made the traditional meal. After, Vati read the Christmas Story according to Saint Luke. "Peace on earth." How strange those words sounded now!

We sang the usual Christmas carols and were thankful for our gifts. But the real joy was missing because of the uncertainties of our present life and future. Toward the end of the evening, our parents told us we would take the train to Allenstein the next day to visit our grandparents and Oma Dorchen. Vati had not yet received orders for his next *Wehrmacht* posting, so he wanted to spend this Christmas with the whole family. Who knew where he would be this time next year?

It was a dazzling white Christmas. For protection against the biting temperature, we wrapped our woolen scarves around our faces as we made our way up the hill to the railway station. The train was hardly heated, so we were glad to get out after the short ride. To reach our destination, we had to cross the black iron railroad bridge on foot. From there the Zimmer-Strasse, where Mutti's parents lived, led away to the left, while the Hohenzollerndamm (whose name had been recently changed to the Hermann-Goering-Strasse), where Oma Dorchen, Vati's mother, lived, branched off to the right. I remember well that whenever we arrived at this particular junction, there was always an argument about which grandparents we should visit first.

This time, given Vati's situation, it was clear that we should visit his mother first. She had a nice lunch waiting for us along with a selection of Christmas goodies, still available at the start of the war. We took dinner at Oma Lina's and Opa Ernst's. It was the traditional Christmas meal of goose, red cabbage, and mashed potatoes. The adults drank beer, while, as a special treat for us kids, Oma Lina had bought a delicious alcohol-free malt brew.

The conversation dealt with the news of the day, primarily war news, and questions about our future. No one expressed any joy at the defeat of Poland. "Didn't I tell you last summer"—Vati was speaking to Opa Ernst—"that the government would run out of money with all those fancy building projects, special programs for the workers, award cruises, and so on? That's why Hitler has started this war, in order to ransack other nations. That's the real reason, believe me! Who knows where he will strike next? Every one of us will have to pay a bloody price for all this one day."

"Didn't we live quietly and in harmony with our Polish neighbors after the *Abstimmung* in 1920? Many of my old school chums have Polish surnames and German first ones like Walter, Werner, Bruno, etc. Some conservative Poles were even permitted to publish newspapers in their own language. This unfortunate war has killed the last hope for future cooperation between our two countries and even for our existence in this land."

"Come on, Hans!" Opa replied. "This is not an appropriate topic for the Holidays. Besides, you paint everything too black."

Vati shook his head. "Black is black. You can't

make it any blacker."

I felt uneasy as I listened to this conversation, so I left the table to play with Hansi. He always seemed to enjoy my company in his bird fashion. Chirping, he flew to the top of my head.

35

New Year's Eve, 1939

Vati, who came home for New Year's Eve, changed into his civilian clothes. Trying to pretend that not too much had changed in our lives, we all dressed up in our best gowns. I admired Mutti's long, flowing, black-silk skirt topped with a long-sleeved pink-taffeta blouse which she gathered in front in a kind of butterfly design—a creation of her friend Grete—and held it all together with a sparking clip in the middle.

The Albrechts were once again invited, since he had not yet been drafted. He was still considered indispensable as a math teacher at the Boys' Gymnasium [academic high school] and the Officers' Academy.

This time there was no carp available. Each household now had ration stamps for meat, dairy products, and a variety of groceries. Mutti had nonetheless managed to prepare a tasty goulash with canned green peas on the side. Frau Albrecht had brought a home-made cake for dessert. And thanks to Vati's foresight, which had caused him to make a large purchase at the beginning of the war, there was still wine on the table. Gerda and I had home-made cherry juice.

Our parents enjoyed being together again with their friends and exchanging the latest about the goings-on in their lives. When the conversation turned political, however, the mood changed, especially when the topic of the Jews came up.

"I wonder where my school friend Mulle Flath is now." Mutti said. "I met her in summer in Allenstein for the last time, when she asked me to visit her secretly in her house. She told me in confidence that she and her family would be leaving the next day for Poland. Handing me a package of new linen, she said, 'Please take it, Trude. I'd much rather you had it than the people who will be taking over our house.' Hugging and crying, we said goodbye. The feeling was indescribable." Mutti lowered her head.

"Surely it is not the first time that the Jews have had to leave a country," Herr Albrecht said, picking up the conversation. "In earlier times they were forced out of Spain, France, England, and other countries and couldn't take their possessions with them then either."

Sadly Vati nodded his head. "So, Bruno, you seem to think it's all right for this to happen and that now it's simply Germany's turn, even though we consider ourselves a civilized and progressive people. The Jews have lived peacefully among us as neighbors, classmates, merchants, doctors, lawyers, etc. for years and had the best treatment of any nation in Europe during the time of the Kaiser."

"Hans, that was not what I meant when I talked about the earlier persecution of the Jews. Of course, it can't be justified for that reason. But the masses are fed the propaganda lies in the *Stuermer*, where they are told that the German people were wronged and mistreated at the end of World War I because of the treachery of the Jews on the home front. That's why so many simply close their eyes and say nothing. Meanwhile, the younger generation is totally brainwashed."

Vati poured wine into the ready glasses, while Mutti motioned us to clear the table and take the dirty plates into the kitchen. There we found Ilse Albrecht cutting the cake. Mutti asked me to take the bowl of whipped cream to the table. As we all spooned away at this delicious dessert, Vati began to talk again. "It looks like my office will be transferred to Allenstein in the course of the new year. We haven't been told the date yet, but I certainly hope it happens."

When we clinked our glasses together at midnight, our eyes locked as we wished each other a healthy new year, one free of harm. Would there be room for some happiness too? I sure hoped so. As someone opened the window and loud radio music blasted out into the night, I started dancing, clapping my hands, and jumping around in an effort to chase all the surrounding gloom away.

Since Great Britain had declared war on us, every house had to cover all its windows with thick, black cloth after sundown. It took a while, though, before we experienced the first air raids. Every neighborhood, moreover, had appointed air-raid wardens who went around at night to check that not even the tiniest sliver of light got through. However, we country people still felt quite secure.

Rations for clothing and shoes were also distributed. I got Gerda's hand-me-down clothes, while Mutti bought me the best leather shoes available. She made sure they were one size larger, since I was a growing child, as she said. For the same reason, I got a pair of sandals, the open fronts of which made it possible to keep them for a long time. Gerda was given new shoes too, but her feet had stopped growing. In our family people had small feet relative to their height.

One afternoon I ran into Annemie coming from town. She was carrying bulging shopping nets. "Don't worry," she laughed. "They are a lot lighter than they

132

look." Her mother had sent her to buy all the wool she could find. "In future we'll probably have to knit all our own socks and sweaters, since any available textile goods will be confiscated by the military," her mother had said.

When Marga came to visit, she always snuck us in some fresh eggs in her handbag. By this point, farmers were no longer permitted to sell their products directly to the public. They had to deliver all produce to the nearest market, which of course was controlled by the government. With all these new regulations keeping us on our toes, the first quarter of 1940 flew by.

36

Rektor Grawen

When school began as usual in the first week of September, I was glad to be back. Fraeulein Sonnabend—her name in English means "Saturday"—asked us to gather and press an assortment of leaves and flowers. These we carefully placed above their names in a special notebook for biology class. I already knew most of them from my hikes with Vati back in Kaltenborn.

For German she asked us to pick a fairytale to act out in class. Each of us had to choose a character and write appropriate dialogue for it in our own words. We all chose *Aschenputtel*—Cinderella. Some girls had trouble with the writing, but I had fun coming up with the right words for the mean stepsisters and their mother. My classmates liked what I had written so much that they wanted to play those characters. As a result, I ended up writing Cinderella's lines and was chosen for the part. I did not think I was pretty enough. Besides, I felt she should be played by a girl with light-blond hair, since that was how she was depicted in all our fairytale books. Fraeulein Sonnabend smiled however and said that that was not important.

The German version of "Cinderella" doesn't have a fairy godmother. The girl simply goes into the garden, shakes a little tree, asks it to send down gold and silver to adorn her drab garments, and it fulfills her wish. Meantime, her shoes are miraculously changed into shining slippers. As in the Disney version, a big pumpkin becomes her coach, and the little mice are transformed into her coachmen. At this point, I should note that the old Germanic tribes worshipped trees, so a magic tree able to rain down treasure may reflect something of our pre-Christian past.

Anyway, the class's performance was a success. What I mainly remember was how entranced I was when I shook the large tree branch stuck in an oversized flowerpot and how for a moment, with my long hair flowing over my shoulders, I really felt beautiful.

These were happy days, almost too good to be true. Unfortunately, that proved to be the case when one day Fraeulein Sonnabend didn't show up for class. We assumed she was ill and wondered who would be the substitute. Suddenly, the door opened, we rose, and a slender middle-aged man entered the room.

"Heil Hitler!" He said. "Good morning, class. I am Rektor Grawen [*Rektor* is principal, and "Grawen" is pronounced "Grah-ven"]. I will be your teacher today because Fraeulein Sonnabend is ill and has to stay home."

"His name was Grabowsky before he changed it not too long ago," my neighbor whispered. Looking at him intensely, I wondered if he were the same Grabowsky who had been Vati's predecessor in Kiefernberg.

He asked us what the last song was we had learned, and, without further ado, we began singing:

> *Wenn die bunten Fahnen wehen*
> *Geht die Fahrt wohl uebers Meer . . .*

[When the bright flags flutter,
Off we sail across the sea . . .]

"Very good," he said, motioning us to stop after the second verse. "Now I need to get to know you all by name," he continued. "Let's start with that row over there." The girls—here in my new school we had separate classes for boys and girls—obediently rattled off their names until he stopped one small girl with short, brown hair in the middle row and asked, "What was your name again?"

"Eva Zimmermann" came the uncertain reply.

With an attempt at an endearing smile that came out crooked, he stepped forward to have a closer look. "When did you and your family move here?" He asked abruptly.

Eva looked at him dumbfounded, her mouth agape, not understanding why he was questioning her in that way.

"What's the matter with you? Can't you speak?" He demanded rather harshly.

In a flash I knew the person he was looking for. When I saw the girl shaking all over, unable to respond, I could not stand it any longer. Taking a deep breath, I raised my hand. He turned toward me: "Yes? What do you want?"

"Herr Rektor, that is not the Zimmermann you are looking for. I am Hannelore Zimmermann from Kiefernberg."

"Oh is that so?" He stepped over to my desk. As he stared down at me with surprise, his phony smile disappeared. Looking him straight in the eye, I wondered why he was so interested in my family's whereabouts and why anger was lurking in his voice. Quickly he turned around, picked up and opened a book from a nearby desk. Then he pointed to different pupils and asked them to read a paragraph out loud. Soon enough it was my turn. I knew that I could read well, but for him my effort was not good enough.

"I can't hear you! Read louder!" He shouted. His presence right behind me was intimidating. Then slamming the book shut with a bang and emitting a nasty laugh, he quipped, "You obviously need lots of practice." Despite what he said, I knew that I had read as well as the other girls, whose performances he had passed over without comment. Although Grabowsky was a good-looking man, when he smiled or laughed he somehow became ugly.

Then he asked us fourth-graders to open our notebooks and practice cursive handwriting [*Schoenschrift*]. At the time it was still done in the old Germanic style of lettering called Gothic. Not to worry, Grabowsky assured us. Soon we would be learning to write cursive with Latin letters. After that he turned his attention to the fifth-graders, with whom we shared the classroom, and gave them a dictation.

It was Saturday—we had school on Saturday mornings in Germany back then. After the first two hours we had gym and outdoor activities. What a relief it was to get out of that classroom and breathe some fresh air!

At lunch I related this incident to my parents. I was still wondering why Rektor Grawen had behaved so unpleasantly to me.

"I can't believe this!" Mutti exclaimed, turning toward Vati. "He must think you had something to do with his removal from the Kiefernberg School. He probably had his eye on the rektor's job, hoping to get it when Tybussek retired. For the real reason for his removal he should probably ask himself!" Mutti laughed. "Now, thanks to his faithfulness to the Party line, he has made a much greater leap by being named the rektor of the considerably bigger Horst Wessel School. What with his name change, he is now 150% German!"

Poking around at my food, I thought all that had nothing to do with me. I was just one of the kids in the class, a fourth-grader. It seemed so unfair that he would take out his frustration and anger on me. That was hardly proper behavior for a teacher, let alone a rektor.

I hoped Grabowsky would stay away from our class in future. Alas, it was not to be! Time and again he found some pretext to visit us, even when Fraeulein Sonnabend was present. On such occasions he would ask her to fill in for some other teacher.

I thought I would get used to his stationing himself behind me when he made us do exercises, but it simply became more and more irritating, even when I tried to imagine him standing there in his underwear as one of my classmates had suggested. One morning he made a point of giving us a dictation from the Fifth Grade reader, which had more difficult words that we had not yet studied. All of a sudden my hands began to tremble, and big, black ink blots fell onto my paper. Never mind, I thought to myself. I would somehow tough it out to the end. I hoped against hope that he would not notice my paper, but of course he did. Gleefully holding my notebook up for the whole class to see, he remarked, "This is Hannelore's work of art. Interesting, isn't it!" The girls giggled and laughed. Whether or not I had made a mistake on the dictation didn't seem to matter to him today. He had found a better way to make me feel ashamed.

By this point I didn't care what happened anymore. Instead, I looked out the window where the last flowers of summer with their ardent colors were celebrating this warm

138

autumn day. A line from a folksong went through my head: *Geh aus mein Herz und suche Freud*—"Go forth, my heart, and look for joy. . . ." I reflected on how nature, which is always kind and accepting, consoles us. It seemed to me that only human beings had the capacity to act in deliberately unkind ways.

Since both my parents worked such long hours and came home so tired, I generally did not to burden them with my Grabowsky encounters. Tonight, however, I was unable to keep this latest incident to myself. So, after Vati and Mutti had finished their conversation about the unsuccessful Battle of Britain and how the spirit of the English people had remained unbroken despite Germany's constant bombardment of their cities, I spilled out my story and expressed how embarrassed I had felt.

My parents did not respond for some seconds while deep lines formed on Vati's forehead. Then he looked at me and smiled. "Don't worry too much about this man. He's basically a poor, ridiculous character. I will think of a solution. Just hang on a little longer." I did, and for a while I was spared any other visitations by Rektor Grawen.

37

A Ray of Sunshine

One day at school, a girl I had recently befriended rushed up to me. Waving a newspaper clipping, she said with excitement, "I have something for you, Hannelore. Read it!"

The clipping turned out to be an announcement from the Treudank Theater. The directors were looking for boys and girls to take part in the upcoming Christmas performance of the "Nutcracker." "Interested youth were to "show up with one parent for auditions at the Ballet Hall the following Wednesday at 5 p.m."

"Oh my," I thought. "Wednesday is tomorrow! I hope Vati has time to take me there."

"Thank you," I gasped, breathless from this exciting news which had entered my world like a ray of sunshine bursting through the dark clouds that had been oppressing me.

The next day I could not get home fast enough after school. While hastily spooning down Oma's chicken soup, I tried to figure out what to wear to the audition. Then I went into the bathroom and washed myself from tip to toe with Vati's fragrant soap.

Oma Dorchen's bathroom, by the way, was the best feature in the apartment. All the fixtures were made of brass or copper, and even the long white bathtub was elevated on little brass feet. The water was gas-heated. Mutti had once explained that when the building was erected in the early 1900's, the architects had used the very best materials then available. By that point the town could already claim a natural-gas pipeline, a functioning clean-water system, good sewage and power systems, and a modern streetcar network. The first train arrived in Allenstein in November 1872, and thereafter the town became an important hub in East Prussia for the national railway. About 20 years later, both my grandfathers were transferred to Allenstein as railway engineers. Anyway, we enjoyed all these modern conveniences after years of living in the country.

After I helped Oma clear the dishes, I excused myself to go to the armoire—to this day Germans tend not to have walk-in closets—and selected my best Sunday dress, the one with the pleated skirt. I next brushed and braided my hair, not forgetting to adorn it at the end with my big pink ribbon.

At 4:30 I was waiting outside Vati's office. What was taking him so long today? I thought as I impatiently walked back and forth. I couldn't have asked Mutti to accompany me, because she always went food shopping right after work and wouldn't be available.

It was ten minutes to five when Vati, smiling, finally appeared. "Vati, we are going to be late now!" I said, almost crying. "The ballet hall will be filled to capacity by the time we get there.

"Don't worry, *mein Kind.* We'll make it," he said, walking off with his long strides while I ran to keep up with him.

I was right. The room was packed when we arrived. We could barely find space to stand in the back near the exit. In the front under bright lights was a group of boys and girls that had already been selected. I started to panic when the ballet master announced that only one more girl was needed. With the same determination that I had shown as the four-year-old snowflake back in Kaltenborn, I pushed my way through the crowd until I stood in one of the front rows, from where I stared at the ballet master intensely. My big ribbon must have caught his attention, since the girls were being chosen for the role of dolls in the performance.

When he pointed to me and asked that I come forward, my heart leaped with excitement. I could hardly believe it.

"Now show us if you can dance," he said. "Just follow the music." The pianist started playing a waltz, and a woman dancer demonstrated the steps. But I really didn't need any instruction. I whirled around, moving my arms to the music, and got so lost in the dance that when the music stopped, I just kept going. Suddenly I looked around. People were laughing and clapping. Herr Arkov—that was the name of the ballet master—came over and took my hand. Smiling, he said, "You've got the part."

Where was Vati? I looked around until I found him grinning from ear to ear, still standing in the back of the room. I waved to him triumphantly, then motioned that he could go, since I needed to stay to get the rehearsal schedule and any other instructions. On the way home, I felt as if I was walking on air.

"Imagine, Mutti," I shouted as I stormed into the living room. "Soon I'll be dancing on the stage of a real theater!"

Mutti smiled, surprised. Then she reminded me not to neglect my studies. She did not have to worry. In fact, the rehearsals gave me so much joy that I felt more energetic and alert in class than ever and regularly finished my homework in no time.

As dolls we had to learn to walk on our tiptoes and take tiny steps with knees held stiff. At the same time we had to make jerky movements with our heads, hands, and arms in order to look like wind-up toys. It was fun.

I did not even worry when one morning Grabowsky paid our class a visit. He was not in such a good mood. He marched up to the teacher's desk, opened a drawer, and seemed to be looking for something specific. He must have been in a hurry, because when he was about to rush off, he closed the drawer on this left thumb.

"Ouch!" He yelled, as he struggled to open the drawer and extract his finger. Meanwhile, his face had turned ashen with pain. When he finally got his thumb out, it was bleeding. The class watched in stunned silence. "There must be a first-aid kit here somewhere," he managed to say. "Does anyone know where it is?"

Without thinking, I walked forward. Not knowing where to look, I was somehow guided to open a little drawer on the right side of the desk, and surprise! There it was. I took out a little bottle of peroxide, poured some onto a piece of gauze, and daubed his wound with it. Grabowsky winced. Then I took a roll of bandaging material and wrapped his thumb as I had learned from Mutti, with some material around the wrist to keep the bandage from slipping off. Astounded but with a crooked smile, he asked me where I had learned to make such a perfect bandage. It was the most positive thing he had ever said to me. "From my mother," I replied. "She is a trained Red Cross volunteer." There was some satisfaction in my voice, and I smiled too, knowing that I had been given a chance to pay back his nastiness with kindness. That fact was not lost on him, and for a moment he seemed somewhat irritated. In any case, he stayed for only an hour this morning and refrained from picking on me. "Did this mean peace?" I wondered. Time would tell.

A postcard came for Oma Dorchen from Biarritz, France, where Uncle Erich was now stationed. Besides describing the beautiful seashore, he mentioned that in the near future his unit would be returning to the homeland and that he was looking forward to being with his family. Oma's face brightened. I had not seen her that happy for a long time.

A few weeks before Christmas, trainloads of mandarin oranges arrived for us German children. They were a gift from our ally, the Italian Government. Each family was to get a crate. The delicious aroma filled our apartment. I ate one in the morning and one after lunch. Half the crate Mutti saved for the Holidays, to be put in our *Bunten Teller*.

Soon we were ready for the dress rehearsal. It was to take place on a Saturday morning, so I was excused from school. Along with my fellow dolls, I received a short pink dress which perfectly matched my ribbon. Afterwards, we were sent to the make-up room, where light stage make-up was applied, giving us rosy lips and cheeks. It made us feel quite grown up to be seated before a big mirror and be attended to by a professional make-up artist

Before we were sent out onto the stage, Mr. Arkov came over to us. "Listen carefully, girls," he said. "When you go on stage, you'll be hit by bright lights that will make you want to blink. Try not to do that. Also, when you reach your positions, don't try to find your father or grandmother in the audience. Actually, the audience will look to you like a big black hole, so you won't be able to recognize people anyway. Just concentrate on your parts.

Do you understand? "Yes, Herr Arkov" came our shy replies, as we nodded our heads.

It was an overpowering feeling being out there. We did well, with only one girl losing a shoe as we were making our exit. Afterward, someone told us not to worry, that it was a good sign if something went wrong during the dress rehearsal.

In compensation for our work, we all got free tickets to the performance for our families. In my case, Oma Lina, Opa Ernst, Oma Dorchen, and my parents attended. Preparing for the early-evening show I packed my polished shoes, a pair of white cotton socks, a towel, a piece of soap, and a sandwich in my little brown suitcase and left for the theater at four. The walk from Oma's house was only ten minutes. This time I was one of the first children to arrive. The stage hands were already busy walking back and forth with sets, decorations, and costumes. A scent of oil paint, make-up grease, perfume, talcum powder, and sweat pervaded the air. This new world I was entering was so different from the uneasy reality outside.

I was already dressed when the other girls, laughing and chatting excitedly, arrived backstage. Some boys in monkey costumes, true to their roles, were running and clowning around in the long corridor until they were told by the stage manager to stop. Others in red and blue uniforms, the toy soldiers, walked around with an air of importance, not forgetting to check their image in the long wall mirrors from time to time.

When the call finally came for us to take our positions on stage, we girls took each other's sweaty hands. This wasn't rehearsal anymore. This was the real thing. Oh, God!

We were lined up one after the other, our hearts pounding as we stared at the closed curtain before us. At least by now our eyes had gotten used to the spotlights. One could hear the murmuring and coughing of the audience until they were drowned out by the overture. All of a sudden, the curtains parted, actors and dancers moved around, and we were transported into the make-believe world of theater. What an extraordinary sensation it was!

The evening went by as fast as a dream—a dream from which I did not want to awake. A new phase of my childhood had begun. It would be one of the happiest.

In our medium-sized town, plays could run for only a limited time. Longer engagements would have been unprofitable, even if busses brought in audience members from the surrounding countryside. Our theater was nevertheless equipped with a modern revolving stage where a variety of shows—dramas, comedies, operettas, operas, and ballets—were produced throughout the year and sometimes scheduled according to the season. I was happy that our Christmas production had more performances than most. That meant that my sister Gerda, who was expected home for the Holidays, would get to see me on stage. The free ticket would be my special Christmas present for her.

Christmas vacation from school had almost arrived when a photographer showed up to take our school pictures. We were lined up by alphabet, so it took them forever to get to me, what with my last name beginning with a zee. By the time it was my turn, I was bored to tears. We had to sit at our desk with our notebook open and pen poised as if we were going to write something. In my case the flash did not function right away, and when it did, it caught me looking like I felt. When we got the proofs back a few days later, I decided to give mine to Oma Dorchen, who actually liked it and put it in a frame. However, we did not order any copies.

I would have forgotten this incident completely except for the fact that a few days later, just before vacation, we were summoned to the auditorium. At the back of the room was a table with a slide projector. Nearby stood Rektor Grawen with two strange men. We were all curious about what they would show us. At that point, the lights were turned off, and on the big screen up front, one after another, our class photos were shown.

Here and there, a photo was kept up on the screen as Rektor Grawen remarked on an especially fine Germanic head or facial structure to the men beside him. These goings-on were strange and not very interesting. Some of the children giggled. I was close to dozing off in the darkened room when I heard my name and saw my enlarged image on the screen. It remained there for quite some time while Grabowsky remarked on my dull eye expression and the structure of my head and face, which seemed a perfect example of a Slavic-Germanic-Baltic mixture with perhaps something else as well. He then gave a dry, sarcastic laugh.

The girls around me turned their heads and stared. Some laughed, and I felt like dropping to the floor. Afterwards, I could not get out of school fast enough. I didn't want to talk to anyone. Was that Grabowsky's way of thanking me for my recent kindness to him? Oh no, it was the revenge of a mean-spirited man who had been caught and helped in a weak moment by a child he had mistreated. The whole incident must have caused him some embarrassment. In short, my hope for more peaceful interactions with him in future had proved an illusion.

When I got home, I rushed to the big window and

sat down on the cool marble window sill. My fists were still clenched in anger and pain as I looked out at the passersby and tried to rid myself of these disturbing emotions. There was no one at home to talk with about it. I felt so alone. True, Oma Dorchen was sitting in her room, knitting away, but it would have been too hard trying to explain everything to her. She wouldn't have understood anyway, since for her generation, the teacher was above reproach and always right. I thought of Gerda, who must have had similar experiences in Osterode. I was getting scared now.

I looked at the clock. It was 2 p.m., time to leave for the ballet studio. I jumped down with relief. At least I had something to look forward to.

After the first performance, Ivan Arkov asked some of us if we would like to join his ballet class, provided our parents approved. We would study for free, he said, and would be called the "Junior City Ballet." As such, we would take part in future performances about once or twice a month—not just ballets, but operas and operettas as well. That prospect was really exciting, and I managed to persuade my parents. "You will get free tickets for all our performances," I announced with a proud smile.

From then on, whenever I opened the stage door and went in, it was as if I shut the door on all the unpleasantness of our daily lives. For a few hours at least, I could feel free and happy. We learned the five different foot positions of classical ballet at the bar in Ivan's studio. The piano accompaniment made the constant repetition of our exercises enjoyable instead of boring. Gradually our limbs became more flexible from the stretching exercises, and the muscle pain we had experienced at the beginning subsided over time.

Mutti and Vati listened carefully to what I had told them about the picture show at school. Then Vati related the plan he had been working on for the last few weeks.

"I have contacted a lady in town who has been granted permission to open a small private school for children with vision, speech, or other learning problems that require special attention. Her name is Frau Professor Mann. She used to teach at the Girls' Lyceum, but after her husband's death she decided to open this special school in her large apartment, where she could also tutor high-school students in the afternoon.

"When I told her about your school problems with Grabowsky, she agreed to take you in as soon as one of her current students left. The size of her quarters limits how many students she can have. Of course, I still needed to come up with a convincing reason for the authorities, and that wasn't going to be easy. Normal children are required to attend the state-controlled public schools. Private schooling for them is forbidden."

"But Vati, you won't tell them that I have a defect, will you?" I asked with a quivering voice.

"Of course not, my child," Vati answered. I have figured out a way to get around the authorities. Here it is. Last Saturday I got a call from Rektor Pipgorra, who asked to see me, since he needed some help again. After I finished my work for him, I proposed to him that I enroll you officially in his school without your having to show up. The school officials here we'd tell that you had to take the train every morning to Osterode in order to attend school in Kiefernberg. Meanwhile, you'd go to Frau Professor Mann's instead the minute she has space for you. I would also let Pipgorra know the exact date. As a reason I told him that I had heard from reliable sources that the Horst Wessel School would be converted into a military hospital in the near future and that the current pupils would be sent on a weekly basis to different nearby facilities. That of course is a confusing situation for a child who has to prepare for taking her high-school admission test. Plus I added that my wife and I were both working and thus were not around much to assist you with your preparations.

"It took a while for Rektor Pipgorra to answer. From his stern look, I could tell that he was weighing the risk he would be taking if he accepted my proposal. In the end, though, he grinned and complimented me on my clever plan. No doubt he was thinking that he would continue to need my help again from time to time in the future. He was still short-staffed, and the military continued to occupy one of his classrooms. So he agreed but added, 'Make sure your daughter is not caught going the wrong way to the railroad station, ha ha ha!'"

Listening to the end of Vati's report, I became concerned that I might be jumping from the frying pan into the fire. After all, it was not inconceivable that I would run into some of my current classmates on their way to school. Still, I did not think this change would take place all that soon. Also, if the pupils had to go to other facilities weekly, Rektor Grawen would be so busy planning that he wouldn't have time to visit our class. This, at least, was my hope.

When I showed up in January at the Horst Wessel School for the first day of classes after Christmas break, there were placards posted in the entrance way telling each grade what school to attend the next day, because Horst Wessel was being converted to other uses. All this naturally caused a big stir among the other kids, since, unlike me, they had had no advanced warning about the change. The shock for me was that it had happened so soon.

The next day I was to show up at the usual time at the large school facility I could see in the distance from Oma Lina's balcony. I used to watch the children running around outside during recess. Fine! Now I could be a part of them. The classrooms however proved old, dark, and in general not as nice as those in the Horst Wessel School. Moreover, I was now mixed in with children I did not know. Only a few from my old classroom had been re-assigned with me.

In the second week we had to start classes at 2 p.m., which meant that when school was over at 6, it was already pitch dark outside. With some neighborhood girls, I slowly walked home. We all put little iridescent buttons on our coats so that we could be seen. It was a little spooky, and we were glad there was some moonlight.

Four weeks later we were sent to yet another school in the opposite direction from where we lived and in a neighborhood with which I was totally unfamiliar. Mutti accompanied me the first day and showed me where to take the streetcar home. At least some of my former classmates were with me this time, but we did not feel at ease. Even our teachers, who also had to switch schools periodically as we did, seemed uncomfortable and frustrated. Fraeulein Sonnabend I never saw again.

One evening while going home, I walked right into someone, who proceeded to burst out laughing. Apparently he had intentionally attached two iridescent buttons, one on either side of his coat, to make it look as if two people were walking side by side. He thought his successful trick was hilarious. I did not think so at all.

38

Frau Professor Mann

In spring Frau Professor Mann wrote to say she had an opening for me. I could start anytime provided Vati had made the necessary arrangements with Rektor Pipgorra in Kiefernberg. My parents were relieved, but for me it was another drastic change. I could feel new anxiety building up. What kind of person would this Frau Professor be? If she had chosen to teach disabled children, she would probably be a kind and patient lady, I told myself. Well, all I could do was wait and see.

When I first met her, Frau Professor Mann turned out to be quite different from my expectations. To me she resembled one of the comic characters created by our satirical author-artist Wilhelm Busch. Feisty, stout but not small, she had an appearance that commanded respect at first sight. Her black hair was piled up on top of her head in the turn-of-the-century fashion. Her pale, fleshy face framed a short nose pinched by her frameless glasses [pince-nez]. Behind them her small, slightly slanted brown eyes blinked bemused when she greeted me.

She took me by the hand and guided me into the room that would be my classroom for the next year. It consisted of two long tables with narrow wooden benches on either side. At the end of the first bench stood a massive wooden armchair from which she would conduct the lessons. The other table, she explained, was reserved for the pupils who would come after school to be helped with their homework and tutored. In the corner of the room closest to the kitchen stood an old armoire. The only window, directly behind her chair, gave sufficient light in the morning, but the view out to the empty courtyard was anything but pleasant. All in all, not a very inviting atmosphere, I thought.

"You will start tomorrow, my child," she said with a strong voice. "But when you come to my door [it was on the second floor], please don't ring the bell. Just use the little brass knocker to the left, and Klara, my housekeeper, will let you in. Remember. No ringing!"

"Yes, Frau Professor Mann," I whispered.

The next morning I left home with mixed feelings. Looking to the left and right, I was concerned that I would meet some girls from my old class. Thankfully, that did not happen. So then I began worrying how I would perform in my new school and with my new teacher. My heart beat faster with every step. Fortunately, the bank where Mutti was working was right across the street from the Frau Professor's building. As I was about to enter my new school, I saw Mutti with a smile waving her encouragement from the big bank window. Tears welling up in my eyes, I took a deep breath, went into the building, and when I reached the door, signaled my arrival as instructed with the brass knocker.

"Come in. Come in, my child." It was Frau Professor Mann herself, smiling, who greeted me at the door. "Here is your seat next to Waltraud, and here are your books. Do you have enough notebooks?"

"Yes, Frau Professor."

And so began the first day of what turned out to be a positive new learning experience—one that was challenging and ultimately rewarding.

At first I did not understand Waltraud because of her nasal speech defect, but soon I got used to how she spoke and could understand her very well. The boy with the club foot was smart but did not speak much, while the boy next to him, who had a vision problem, was always struggling with reading. Despite her strictness, Frau Professor Mann proved very patient with them, and before long I began to like her. I did not even mind when she called me *Wuerstchen*, Little Sausage, whenever I did not answer fast enough for her when we were dealing with my nemesis, math problems. (It only figures that mathematics would be my downfall, given that Vati was a near-genius in the field!)

"But Frau Professor," I answered back one day. "You always tell us to think carefully before we speak."

She chuckled, amused. "Well, Wuerstchen, just try to think faster next time."

"Ja, Frau Professor."

39

What Real Prayer Is Like

For the Christmas Season this year, Ivan Arkov, the ballet company director, had planned a big performance. He had us learn a very solemn piece called "The Praying Choir Boys" as well as a playful dance tableau based on a 17th-Century pastoral scene. Both pieces had appropriate music and costumes. Our routine after-school ballet training became very intense during this time to prepare us fully for the forthcoming performance. Still, it was fun, and we all wanted to do our best.

In the midst of all this, I came down with tonsillitis and the accompanying fever. I seemed to be getting this sort of illness more and more recently. I had to stay in bed with wet wraps and woolen scarves around my neck. Mutti was a firm believer in this treatment, especially when combined with the regular doses of aspirin. And she wasn't wrong. It worked.

One morning while I was still recovering—it must have been a Sunday, since everyone was home—I was awakened by a loud radio bulletin: Japanese warplanes without warning had attacked the U.S. naval base at Pearl Harbor in Hawaii as well as assorted British outposts in the Pacific. Everyone was in shock. The day was December 7, 1941. I was not quite eleven years old. Four days later, Germany and Italy declared war on the United States, and Vati wasn't the only one upset this time. What would happen next?

Indeed, so much had taken place in the world during the year now ending, but I had been so busy tending to my own worries that I was barely aware that the German Army had invaded Denmark, Norway, Greece, and Yugoslavia. We now seemed to be everywhere, even in North Africa. At the moment, though, I was more concerned with getting well and not missing any more rehearsals.

Another war bulletin that came through during lunch around this same time period was less foreboding and even caused us to laugh in spite of the tragedy taking place all around us: "A big herd of African elephants obviously sided with our German troops," the announcer reported with a chuckle. "They defended their territory against the Brits by charging them. With their large ears pointed and trumpeting as they went, they attacked in force. The panicked Brits barely managed to escape with their vehicles and their lives."

Getting back to our Christmas performance, I had a profound experience on opening night. We were positioned sideways to the left and right at the top of a broad staircase. Behind us was a huge gothic window illuminated from behind. This backdrop had the effect of throwing different-colored rays through the sections of supposed stained glass. Ivan Arkov had selected an adagio movement from a classical piece, which we followed with slow, gentle hand movements. We lifted our arms up as if in prayer, then slowly we walked to the middle where we met our partners from the other side. Then, turning toward the audience with our arms at our sides and open palms facing front, we carefully descended the steps. We had to look straight ahead and were not to look down at our feet. That was quite a difficult task for us, since we were dressed in long, white gowns with black tunics on top. During dress rehearsal one of the taller girls had stumbled and almost fallen down the steps. The managing director had one of his tantrums. The upshot was, her dress was shortened that day.

We also had to wear pageboy wigs. Mine was strawberry blond. I hardly recognized myself in the mirror.

When we reached the last two steps, we lifted our arms upward towards the lights and turned to one side again when we reached the bottom of the stage, where we slowly kneeled down in prayer while continuing to look up.

Precisely at this moment I felt a shiver run down my spine, and a quiet sensation beginning in my heart extended to my arms and legs. It was something I had never felt before, as if I were connected with something beyond the lights. From that instant on, I knew what real prayer was.

We slowly walked back up the stairs to our starting positions, where we stood motionless like statues. When the curtain fell, there was a moment of silence followed by an explosion of applause. Ivan Arkov was clever. He knew what would appeal to the citizens of our predominantly Catholic town. The managing director was very pleased with our performance. Leaning out of his booth stage left, he demonstratively clapped his hands.

I stayed in the wings for a while to watch the next number, a pas de deux which paired Ivan with one of the adult female dancers. It was called *"Der Tod und das Maedchen"* ["Death and the Maiden"]. In the midst of their dance, a shrill ringing swept through the theater. What was that? *Fliegeralarm!* [Air-raid warning!] "Everyone to the basement!" The managing director shouted. We all ran downstairs as fast as we could.

Most of the people in the audience went to the

theater restaurant, which was on the basement level. As I made my way through the corridor, I heard Mutti's voice from a distance. She was asking a man, "Where is my daughter? Has someone seen her?" I ran towards her. "Here I am, Mutti," I said, looking up at her. But thanks to my reddish-blond wig, she didn't recognize me at first. I laughed.

"Oh, is that your daughter?" The man said, turning to Mutti.

"My God," I gasped. "It's the managing director."

"I watched her closely on the stage," he continued. She was totally absorbed in her performance. She has real talent." Blushing, I hid behind Mutti's back.

The alarm had not lasted very long, and nothing had happened. The show could go on. Off and on, we had similar false alarms. The rumor even went around that we got them whenever Hitler's motorcade was passing through town on the way to or from the Wolfschanze, his well-camouflaged East Prussian hideaway. That way no one would be in the streets, since his assistants had not forgotten that his limousine had been stoned during his one and only visit to Allenstein. But these were only speculations. The truth was that on several occasions enemy planes had been spotted circling over the forest. They had even been seen to drop red and green ball-shaped observation lights. Still, it had proved impossible for them to find any structures in the dense woods below.

40

A Visit from
General von Luettwitz

Vati had heard that one of the stores in town had received a shipment of canned stewed tomatoes from Italy. He thus went there every day and returned home with two canvas Army bags stuffed to the breaking point. On one such evening a suspicious neighbor stopped him and asked what he was carrying in those heavy bags. She doubtless suspected that Vati was involved in the black market. He simply laughed and opened one of the bags. The woman was shocked. "Everyone can purchase these downtown." He told her. "We'll store them for the winter when we'll most need Vitamin C."

"Ach, what a good idea!" The now embarrassed woman replied. "We must get some too." Then she turned and quickly walked back to her house.

Good food became scarcer and scarcer as the war went on. Housewives had to become very creative when it came to cooking. Everything now required waiting in line, even vegetables. Vati was a big man, and he must have been hungry most of the time, especially for protein.

One day he came up with a clever idea. He had heard that a butcher in town was looking for a math tutor to help his son pass the high-school entrance exam. Vati got the job and took me with him when he visited the boy's house on Saturday afternoons. "These extra lessons will be good for you too," he said. I did not mind, because after the sessions we were always invited to stay for a dinner of frankfurters or Viennese sausages with home-baked bread.

Vati had asked to be paid with meat or meat products, to which the family agreed. So for a while we had an additional supply which nicely supplemented our meager meat rations. Often, the butcher threw in some soup bones which Mutti used thrice over to enrich her vegetable soup.

One day a funny situation came up in my illegal private school that Vati had arranged to get me out of Rektor Grawen's clutches. It was around noon, the time when most of the high-school students dropped by for tutoring. Suddenly we heard the shrill ringing of the front doorbell.

Frau Professor Mann, our teacher, was livid. *"Du Ganskopf!* [You goosehead!] How often must I tell you not to ring that bell?!"

Then we heard the tell-tale steps of someone wearing boots followed by the metallic sound of heels being clicked smartly together. There in the doorframe appeared the tall figure of a distinguished-looking older officer with an Iron Cross hanging around his neck.

"Excuse me, honored Frau Professor Mann, my name is von Luettwitz*, and I have come to pick up my son Fritz, as I am in town for a brief visit. Is he here?"

Frau Professor Mann jumped up from her chair as if she had been stung by a wasp. Displaying her most

*Baron Smilo von Luettwitz (1896-1969), born in Neuburg on the Danube, Bavaria, was known as a general who "led his men from the front." A lieutenant general, he was named commander of the German Panzer [Tank] Corps on November 1, 1944. (Source: www.vktraeger.de/Personenregister.)

charming smile, she rushed into the corridor. "Ah, Herr General, I am so sorry! I thought it was one of the kids!" With that, she motioned him into her drawing room.

Fritz was surprised too. Seeing his father, the boy gave him a mock salute as the General disappeared into the other room. Jumping on top of a cupboard near the kitchen door, he used his ruler as his microphone and in his best radio-broadcaster High German Fritz intoned, "Today in the City of Allenstein at Wilhelmstrasse 20, General von Luettwitz and the Russian Foreign Minister Molotov have begun top-secret meetings to exchange ideas and a considerable amount of schnapps. Let's hope that their negotiations will eventuate in a peaceful settlement!"

Then Fritz jumped back to his seat and buried his head in a book. We all giggled. It struck me at that moment that the comparison between Molotov, whose picture I had often seen in the newspaper, and Frau Professor Mann was not all that far-fetched. Somehow she really looked like a female version of Molotov with piled-up hair.

Fritz always played the class clown, and he usually got Frau Professor Mann to laugh. He was a smart kid but needed a firm hand. That was why his mother had sent him to Frau Professor Mann's. That way he would be forced to do his homework. Because of the War, his father was often absent for long periods and thus could not help teach the boy good study habits.

More than a half hour had passed since the unexpected arrival. When Frau Professor Mann returned to the classroom, she motioned for Fritz to join his father in the corridor. Then, after some more saluting and heel clicking, General von Luettwitz and his son made their exit.

Sitting closest to Frau Professor Mann, I noticed

her heavily alcohol-scented breath. For a while she sat very still, nervously drumming the table with the long fingernails of her left hand She had white, fleshy hands, and as a widow she followed the tradition of wearing two golden wedding bands, her own and her husband's, on her left ring finger.

We looked at her attentively, waiting for our next assignment. When she moved her lips, however, something different and strange came out: "One day many heads will roll down the Kaiser Wilhelm Allee! Rolling, rolling. . . ." And she accompanied these words with a circling motion of her hand.

Oh God, how creepy! I felt like running away. A second later, composed and back to her old self, she gave us our homework assignments.

In recent years I had gotten used to hearing ambiguous and often scary statements at home. Like them, I hid this one too in a secret drawer of my mind.

41

Denying God

I t was the Friday before Pentecost, our last day of school before vacation. We had only four hours of classes—German, history, geography, and religion. I still remember the big map of the Soviet Union hanging in the front of our classroom. As I looked at the vast expanse of that country, the world's largest, the voice of the teacher faded from my attention. Wondering if the German Army would ever be able to conquer Russia completely, I suddenly saw in my mind's eye the red pinheads on Vati's map retreating toward our border. The thought made me shudder. What would happen to us then? For a second I felt panic, but the clanging school bell chased it away.

At this point the old pastor walked in. Asking us to open our school Bibles, he began to read from one of the Gospels. He followed up with passage-by-passage explanations. As always, I was absorbed by the contents while most of my classmates, disinterested, were working surreptitiously under their desk tops on their homework.

I was moved by the wonderful stories about the compassionate, gentle, and at the same time powerful Son of God. Unfortunately, all that had taken place a long time ago, and not much seemed to have changed for the better in the world in the interim. From where I sat, I could look out the big classroom windows and see all the church steeples in town—five or six Catholic churches and one small Protestant one. People had prayed there day after day for hundreds of years, yet hostilities without end had gone on between neighbors of different denominations not to mention between countries. Christ was even betrayed by his followers, and over the centuries people had failed to take to heart and act on his simple message: "Love one another, forgive one another." Was the Kingdom of God only a fairytale?

For quite some time I had denied the existence of God and had felt a big vacuum inside me but was afraid to talk about it to anyone. Mutti and Vati were so busy; they went to church on only the big holidays. They would often say that it was enough to pray at home in one's own room as Jesus himself had advised. Moreover, I saw them frequently acting charitably toward the people around us. Oma Lina was the one family member who was a regular churchgoer. However, I felt shy about sharing my problem with her. I did not want to upset her, since she already had her hands full with Tante Hanna.

I began having nightmares from which I would awake with rapid heartbeat and shortness of breath. Vati and Mutti would come into my room, hold me, and bring me a glass of cold water. When they consulted our family doctor, he interpreted my disturbed sleep as pre-adolescent symptoms that would go away with time.

Now on this particular Friday as I was leaving school, conflicting emotions were welling up in me. On the one hand, I wanted Jesus' positive message to be true, but on the other, I still could not believe in God. I was walking with a friend, whose conversation I half listened to in an absent-minded way. As we passed a big yellow church near Oma Dorchen's street, the feeling suddenly arose in me to run up the stone steps, enter the sanctuary, and walk quickly down the aisle. Stopping at the first row of pews, I spontaneously reached for several prayer books and flung them without thinking toward the altar. Then I ran as fast as I could back to the entrance, where my friend was waiting.

"What were you doing in there?" She asked, disturbed.

"Just something I had to," I replied, waving away further questions.

Parting at the next intersection, we wished each other a nice vacation. As I was waiting for the cars to clear so I could cross the street, something unexpected happened. I seemed to hear a voice, not mine, talking softly to me from inside: "You are still a child," it said. "But soon you will be grown up and responsible for whatever you do. Be careful!"

It was as if I had been struck by lightning. In shock and without looking to the left or the right, I ran toward our apartment building, up the stairs, and straight into my room. Breathless, I cowered in the corner on the floor and began to shake all over. I was overcome by a feeling of fear and remorse. Why had I done that? I had no answer.

I stayed in my position on the floor until my parents got home. By then I noticed that big red blotches had begun to form on my arms and legs.

"Hans, call the doctor right away," Mutti said. "I think she's coming down with something. She has a temperature."

Shivering from waves of fever, I was put to bed and given aspirin. Even the big, fluffy down comforter did not warm me up. The window was covered with dark blankets, as always, to keep light from being seen from outside. "Sleep tight," Mutti said, tucking me in. "You'll feel better tomorrow." Then I was alone.

I tried to fall asleep, but as weak and tired as I was, I couldn't. My head was throbbing, my checks felt hot, and my body continued to shiver. Before long I heard the grinding of the door. I wanted to see who was there, but my eyelids were too heavy to open. I heard whispering and recognized Oma Dorchen's voice: "Herr Doktor, what is your diagnosis?"

"It's a clear case of measles," came the answer. "But if her high fever doesn't go down, I doubt that she'll make it through the night. Please check on her from time to time."

Then I heard them leave the room. Alone again in the dark, I thought, "What did the doctor say? I might not make it through the night. But that's impossible! I'm too young to die!"

"Nobody's too young to die," came the unbidden voice inside me.

With that a dialogue began within me.

"It was awful what I did today," I told the voice. "I don't know why I suddenly got so angry. It was terrible. I promise I will never do anything like that again. I am so sorry. Please let me live. I still have so much I want to do in my life. I want to live!"

I felt my body getting lighter and lighter. It was as if it were beginning to move upwards of its own accord. I got scared. Summoning up whatever energy I had left, I lifted my arms and grabbed the cool brass bars of the bedstead behind me. With my last strength I pulled myself down and down. After that there was nothingness.

The next thing I remember is opening my eyes. I was still in my room! "Mutti, Mutti," I cried. "Where are you? I'm hungry!"

Smiling, she looked through the partially opened door. *"Guten Morgen, mein Kind!* ["Good morning, my child."] You've slept for a long time. Let me just check your temperature," she said, slipping the thermometer under my tongue. "My goodness," she added a few minutes later. "It's almost all gone."

"Yes, Mutti." I gave her a little smile. "But now I need to eat something and drink something too."

Before long, Mutti had returned with a cup of slightly warm linden tea sweetened with honey—an old country remedy—and a small bowl of oatmeal with milk and honey, sprinkled lightly with cinnamon. How good it tasted! Then I took a spoonful of the medicine prescribed by the doctor and washed it down with the leftover tea.

Mutti explained that the room had to be kept dark when someone had the measles; otherwise the daylight might harm their eyesight. I noticed that while she was talking, she kept a good distance from my bed and shook her head doubtfully: "This is so strange. I'm sure you had the measles as a toddler. No one gets them twice, they say. Well, I guess you are just a special girl!" With that, she left the room.

I blushed. How could I tell my parents about yesterday? How would they understand when I couldn't myself? Better keep this to myself for now. Everyone most likely had some kind of secret they carried around with them, I reasoned. Plus, hadn't I already received my punishment? Still, I felt bad that I had probably ruined the family's Pentecost vacation. Anyway, when the time was right, I would tell them all about it. As it happened, that took years.

I had a speedy recovery, and soon the memory of what I had done seemed to fade away like a bad dream.

Nevertheless, I had missed valuable time during the last weeks of school and was busy catching up with extra homework to make sure I got a good year-end report card. I also did not want to miss our regular exercise routines in the ballet studio. My illness, however, had lowered my overall energy, and the good food I needed to become strong had grown scarce as the war years went on.

Recently a new girl had joined our ballet class. We happened to have been together at the Horst Wessel School. The year before she had entered a middle school where Herr Grawen (Grabowski) was the new principal. Smiling, she told me that Rektor Grawen remembered me. "Just the other day he dropped the remark that a certain Hannelore Zimmermann never seemed to know what school she wanted to attend."

I couldn't believe it. Even from afar, this man refused to leave me alone. He had probably found out I had entered the Luisen Lyceum and knew from the records that this girl and I were old classmates from elementary school and possibly still in touch. How I had hoped never to hear his name again. Was he planning to try to get me back into his school? But why? This was all very strange and unsettling.

(Above) The Napierski Family in front of their new house built, with Vati's insistence, by the *Arbeitsdienst* (Youth Work Corps); *(below)* Mulle Flath, Mutti's Jewish girlfriend forced to leave East Prussia in the 1930's

(Above top) Kiefernberg Elementary School, 1938; *(above)* the same building, now an agricultural institute, Poland, 1999.

(Above top) School outing, Osterode Lake District, 1939;
(above) General Smilo von Luettwitz.

(Above clockwise) I am the proud seven-year-old flowergirl at Tante Elly's wedding, 1938; I.D. picture, age 13; with my sister Gerda, August 1943; *(opposite top)* Christmas 1943, I'm top right, behind Oma Dorchen; *(opposite lower)* Mutti—the last summer in the homeland, 1944.

Vorzugs=Karte Nr. 1507

Frau ___T h i e l , Gerda___
      Name   Vorname

z.Zt. Buchwalde, Schule
Wohnort und Wohnung

hat Anspruch auf bevorzugte Abfertigung

Dieſer Ausweis gilt vom ___4. 10. 1944___
bis ___für die Dauer der Eva-___
___kuierung in Osterode.___

Bevorzugt abfertigen!

Nicht übertragbar

Osterode
  Ort

4. 10. 1944   Kreisamtsleiter
  Datum

Dieſer Ausweis wird von der NSV. „Hilfswerk Mutter und Kind"
als D A U E R A U S W E I S an kinderreiche Mütter (das ſind Mütter
mit vier und mehr erziehungsbedürftigen Kindern) ausgegeben.

Befriſtet (d. h. auf begrenzte Zeit) wird der Ausweis auf Antrag des
Hilfswerkes „Mutter und Kind" auch in Sonderfällen an andere
Frauen (Schwangere, Berufsgeſchädigte uſw.) ausgegeben.

Ich bitte alle Dienſtſtellen der Partei, des Staates und der Wirtſchaft
(insbeſondere alle Einzelhandelsgeſchäfte), die Inhaberin dieſer Karte
bevorzugt abzufertigen.

NSDAP., Gauleitung Oſtpreußen

Gauleiter.

Nicht übertragbar

Vorzugs=Karte Nr. 1 485

Frau ___Z i m m e r m a n n Gertrud___
      Name   Vorname

Allenstein Herm-Göringstr.
Wohnort und Wohnung

hat Anspruch auf bevorzugte Abfertigung

Dieſer Ausweis gilt vom ___25. April 42___
bis ___bis auf Abruf!___

Bevorzugt abfertigen!

Allenstein
  Ort

25. IV. 42   Kreisamtsleiter
  Datum

(Above) With Struppy—August 1944—five months before leaving for Bavaria; *(opposite from top)* Gerda's I.D. Card—October 1944, signed by Gauleiter Koch, the Nazi governor of East Prussia; Mutti's last I.D. Card in East Prussia.

(Opposite top left-to-right) Me, Mutti, Gerda, and two other "passengers" in front of our Red Cross train—January 1945; *(opposite lower)* the train nurse with the Dutch doctor who saved my life; *(above top)* Mutti's and my "refugee" card in Bavaria, March 20, 1945; *(above)* Mutti with Baby Olaf—Summer 1945.

Me *(above)* and Gerda *(opposite)* at Gruenwald-by-Munich, 1945. I've just turned 14.

(Above top) The Hunting Castle, Gruenwald, Bavaria; *(above)* enroute to Poland with our interpreter, Liesbeth—October 1999; *(opposite from top)* Christine and I—Marga's Garden; in front of Kiefernberg Lake and Christine with swans—Kiefernberg, October 1999

City hall, Allenstein,
East Prussia

My childhood friend, Marga *(center)*,
with husband and grandson in their
garden—Poland, May 2000

42

Surrender at Stalingrad

This year autumn was short. When winter arrived, it came with a vengeance. In early November Dora Hank came to visit. With her was a tall, handsome, uniformed man whom she introduced as her fiancé. They sat quietly on the sofa, holding hands, in the bay-window room until Mutti, Vati, and Gerda came home from work. Later on, they all went out together. I was glad to see Dora so happy. The man did not leave much of an impression on me, however. Their visit was too short.

Classroom work was very demanding again this year. At least we had a great art teacher, a dark-haired young woman whom rumor claimed to be the wife of an officer. She introduced us to water coloring, had us memorize the colors of the rainbow, and taught us how to mix paints in order to create other hues. Our first assignment was to create a picture based on a song we knew well. My choice was *"Heidenroeslein"* ["Little Rose on the Heath"], a poem by Heinrich Heine that had been famously set to music by both Mozart and Schubert. We had to print the verses in the middle of the sheet, then surround them with a colorful painted frame describing the content in visual form.

After painting a light-green-and-yellow background, I created little red roses in each corner. On the upper part of the frame, I sketched the figure of a boy running with outstretched arms toward the flowers. The teacher walked

169

around the room to check on our work. When she got to my desk, she stopped for a moment, nodded, and gave me a knowing smile.

As I write these words, I am again amazed at how I can recall all these special moments from 60-plus years ago as if they had happened in the recent past. As we get older, time seems to contract, as if our minds are not made to contain the full expanse of our years. At least, that's how it seems to me.

One late November afternoon when darkness had come early and it was cold and foggy outside, I was busy creating a jumping jack out of cardboard. It was an art project for class. When I got it back, I would give it as a Christmas present to my little cousin Gitti. Humming along with the radio, I felt happy and comfortable in the warmth of the room. I was just about to paint a colorful suit on the figure when the corridor door burst open, and Mutti, still in her overcoat, rushed in, tears streaming down her face: "Our Army is defeated at Stalingrad. They surrendered to the Russians today. Everything is lost now. How will we ever be able to recover on the Eastern Front in the midst of this severe winter?" With this last sentence, she threw herself down on the bed.

I jumped up from my chair and ran over to her. Vati, meantime, had entered the room and tried to calm her down. "Come on, Trude! It's not the end of the world yet. I agree. Things don't look good for the future. But there's nothing else we can do but struggle on and hope that we'll be spared the worst."

Mutti sat up and dried her face. Suddenly aware that I was in the room, she managed a smile and said, "Yes, my child. Vati is right. We have to be brave and hope for the best." I went over to hug her, but it was more a desperate sort of clinging in an attempt to get rid of the punch I had felt in my stomach when I had heard the news.

A few days later, when Vati came home at night from work, he shook the snow off his overcoat, looked around with a grave expression, and called for Mutti, who was in the kitchen. "Trude, please bring me a cup of hot tea and come in here and sit down. I have to tell you about something that happened today in the office. Both went into the next room and shut the door behind them.

Oh, it must be something serious, I thought, and went into Oma's red room, where the tall door to the bay-window room was never completely closed. Tiptoeing as near to the door as I dared, I heard the following conversation.

"Between ten and eleven this morning, a man walked into my office," Vati began, his voice hardly louder than a whisper. "You can't imagine how dreadful he looked—skin and bones covered by shabby, worn-out clothes. He handed me his identification papers with a shaking hand as he stared at me with large, sunken eyes.

"'Man, you look awful,' I said. 'Where are you coming from?' He simply pointed to the paper where I read 'KZ Buchenwald.'

"'Please sit down while I get you something to drink,' I said. You know, Trude, we always have a pot of herbal tea on the hot plate. So I brought him a cup, placed it in front of him on my desk, went to the door and closed it.

"I waited a few minutes for him to warm up, then began to ask him some questions. 'So you were there as a political prisoner, as I can see from this paper. Why have they released you now?'

"'The doctor in the camp diagnosed me with MS

171

and told me I did not have long to live. I pleaded with him to let me go home to die with my family. My request was granted.'

"'Oh, I see,' I replied. 'But tell me, Herr _____, what exactly goes on in those camps? I have never met anyone who was released from one. We are told that they are work camps pure and simple, but from your appearance I can tell that there is more to it than that. At the very least, they must have had you on a starvation diet, right?'

"The man gave me a long, penetrating look, put his index finger over his mouth, and said, 'My lips are sealed. I am sworn to silence. If I say even a word, they will send me right back. You see, I can't even speak about the camp to my wife, or else I will endanger her as well.'

"I saw a flicker in his eye. He was probably afraid I was testing him to see if he would say something or not. I assured him I was not a Secret Police interrogator but only a small-time Army bureaucrat. Then I stamped his papers to indicate that he had registered with our office and handed them back to him. At that point I wished him a safe trip home and peaceful days with his family. Sighing with relief, he thanked me and quickly left the room."

I heard Mutti's nervous cough, something she had recently developed. Then Vati spoke up again: "There is definitely something rotten in Greater Germany, don't you agree? Not only is this man sworn to secrecy, but I've heard that anyone assigned to work in a camp has to pass certain psychological tests. Unimaginable things must be happening there. I've heard from other sources that anyone who disobeys orders by talking about what goes on in these camps will be shot. That's how low our Government has stooped, and it will take the whole nation down with it. The majority of our people are oblivious to these facts. They are so brainwashed, helpless, or indifferent."

"Oh God, Hans! I don't know what to say. It was bad enough to chase all the Jews out of their homes, but what are they doing with them now when even a German prisoner is in such devastating shape?"

"Yes, Trude, only God knows!"

After that there was a long silence. As quickly as I could, I snuck out to Oma's bedroom. I had heard enough.

43

The 20th of July, 1944

It was a sunny afternoon. With instructions from Gerda on the perfect way to iron a blouse, I found myself behind our ironing board. I would have preferred going for a swim. Fortunately, light radio music kept me entertained as I did my duty. Rosita Serrano, the popular Spanish vocalist, had just begun to chirp her best-loved song (in German), *"Der kleine Liebesvogel singt sein Liebeslied. / Tirilirile, tirilirili, tirilirile. . . ."* ["The little lovebird sings its love song/ Teereeleereelay, teereeleereelee, teereeleereelay."] Suddenly, the music stopped, and an agitated male voice broke in with this bulletin: "Irresponsible, treacherous criminals of high military rank attempted this morning to assassinate the Fuehrer during a briefing with his staff officers at the Wolfschanze. Although the explosives tore the building apart, the Fuehrer, thanks to Providence, managed to escape unharmed except for a few superficial wounds. Some officers standing next to him at the briefing table were seriously wounded, and one was killed on the spot."

I froze, and the hot iron dropped to the floor. Gerda, who had been folding laundry behind me, ran to the radio and turned up the volume, since we had missed the names of the men standing next to Hitler. She turned around toward me. "What smells? Lore, where's the iron?"

I awoke from my stupor. "Here it is," I said, as I

stooped down and grabbed it just moments before it would have burned the carpet.

Mutti had heard the news from the next room and rushed in. "Do they know yet who did it?"

"The newscaster said more information would be forthcoming shortly and that listeners should stand by," Gerda replied.

Later we learned that it was the one-armed Count von Stauffenberg who had placed his briefcase with the bomb underneath the table where Hitler was standing, then excused himself to go outside and call his office in Berlin. As he was walking to his waiting car, he heard the bomb go off and assumed it had done its job. He was able to bluff his way out of the secured compound by saying he was chasing the traitors.

With a sarcastic laugh, the news reporter told how shocked the "Herr Count" was when, on telling Dr. Goebbels back in Berlin that the Fuehrer was dead, the grinning Goebbels handed him the phone and said, "Here, why don't you tell him that yourself!"

Now we knew what the code word *Walkuere* [Valkyrie] meant and who the other officers in the plot to overthrow Hitler were. That night they were all shot, with the exception of a handful of very high-ranking officers, who, per the usual protocol, were given the option of shooting themselves. The one-armed count was not among them.

For a while the three of us sat around the table in a daze. (Frau Annemarie was no longer with us. A week before she had followed her husband to Striegau in Silesia, where the Imperial Patent Office had been transferred, to escape the saturation bombing of Berlin.) We tried to imagine what might have happened had the assassination plot succeeded.

"With the Army adrift without a central leader," Mutti commented, "the Red Army would have been on our doorstep before we knew it. And they would not have shown us any mercy, regardless of the uprising against Hitler."

We also wondered how Vati was doing in his office. Mutti went to the post office to give him a call. She heard that everything there was unchanged, only that a thorough inspection would take place the following week. Therefore, Vati would be unable to come home as planned for the weekend. He had to spend the time preparing.

In school the next day everybody was still upset, the students as well as the teachers. Herr von Knobelsdorf called a special assembly. When we all gathered in the auditorium, he appeared in full uniform and delivered an emotional speech condemning the traitors. Then he gave us, the German youth, a pep talk. The assembly ended with our singing, our right hands extended, the national anthem—*"Deutschland, Deutschland, ueber Alles"* ["Germany, Germany above All Else"]. The rest of the day is a blur.

Later on, we got to hear Vati's opinion. "Those aristocrats should have acted much earlier," he said, shaking his head, "when Hitler betrayed old Chancellor von Hindenburg in 1933 and seized power. Hitler clearly had no intention of restoring the monarchy. Now, at the eleventh hour, it is far too late. Moreover, this handful of men would have been unable to take over the government. There are just too many fanatics around, even among the generals, not to mention the SS. Still, Stauffenberg will be remembered for his desperate act as a tragic hero. So I suppose we'll just have to endure till the end."

A hectic restlessness hung in the air from that day on. The papers were full of man-hunt stories, and gloomy new propaganda posters were suddenly everywhere. They showed a figure in a long, dark overcoat and a broad-brimmed hat pulled down over his eyes. In big block letters one read, *"DER FEIND HOERT MIT!"* ["THE ENEMY IS LISTENING IN!"] From now on, everyone was regarded as a potential traitor, and we all had to be doubly and triply careful about what we did and said and with whom we spent our time.

At the movies, the newsreels made sure to include grim scenes from the makeshift courtroom in Berlin. The prosecutor was screaming at the traitors who were standing in front, holding their pants with both hands, since their belts had been removed to humiliate them and no doubt to keep them from hanging themselves before receiving summary justice from the firing squad.

The Osterode newspaper also reported that enemy paratroopers had recently been spotted landing in the nearby woods. The population was told to practice vigilance, since several field workers had disappeared shortly thereafter. One couldn't be too careful!

44

A Friendly Invitation to a Betrayal

One morning as I was walking to school with a classmate named Margot, she asked if I would like to come over to her house that afternoon. "We have a large garden with berries and fruit trees," she said. "The dark cherries are ripe just now, and you could take some home."

"Sure," I replied. Is 3:30 all right? I have to do my homework first."

"Of course. Any time is fine with me" was Margot's response.

Her house was the tallest and the largest on the main street leading to the lake. It was in fact a mansion. We had fun gathering berries and cherries as we talked about our plans for the upcoming summer vacation. When I told her I needed to go, she shook her head: "No, Hannelore. My mother said you must stay and eat with us. She has prepared a nice meal."

So we went inside and, along with Margot's little sisters, gathered around the large dining table. During the meal the father questioned me about our time in Allenstein, what kind of position Vati had at the Army office, where Mutti worked, and so on. I had nothing to hide but found it a bit odd that he showed so much interest in our family when we hardly knew him. Looking back now, another strange thing is that Margot's parents are among the few people in my past whose faces I cannot recall. They are like shadows in my memory.

The next day it was unseasonably hot. I was glad to get out of the sticky classroom at noon. All of us kids were overjoyed that summer vacation would start in two days.

Margot approached me as I bounded down the stairs. "Hannelore, would you like to go swimming with me in the lake this afternoon? My aunt has a house right on the shore."

"Of course," I said. "I'd love to cool off, but I don't have a bathing suit with me."

"That's no problem," Margot laughed. "I always keep an extra one at my aunt's place. So, come on. Let's go."

We skipped down the steep street to the lake, chatting as we went. When we came to a curve where the street turned to follow the shoreline, Margot stopped and pointed to a little side street that led to a three-story yellow-brick building with a flag in front. "Oh my goodness!" Margot exclaimed. "I almost forgot to deliver this letter to my father that he'd left at home. He works here, you know. Would you mind coming in with me for a moment. It shouldn't take long."

"Of course not," I replied. "We are not in a rush, are we?"

We bounded up the six stone steps and entered the large entrance hall. She led me to an open door on the right, and before I knew it, I was inside with the door shut behind me. Margot had disappeared, but I was not alone. When I looked up, I saw two tall older boys with shining boots in Hitler Youth uniforms. They were staring at me with contempt.

"Why haven't you attended any Hitler Youth meetings since you moved here?" One of them shouted.

"Well, no one invited me" came my lame reply, which seemed to puzzle them.

"Where is your father? What kind of work does he do?" The other one wanted to know. "Is he a criminal?"

I couldn't believe my ears and started to tremble. Meantime, the wheels of my mind were turning rapidly. Do they suspect that Vati is involved in the 20th of July? I thought. Probably.

My heart was pounding very fast now. Nevertheless, I pulled myself together and, staring back at them, answered in the sort of language they were used to.

"My father," I said, "is an honorable soldier in the Germany Army!"

At that moment, a door to my left opened, and two young Band of German Young Women (BDM) women appeared. "Leave her alone," one of them said to the boys. "We'll take care of this case." They motioned me to follow them into the next room. I was led to a small desk near the window and offered a chair. At least they were a little more civil.

A sheaf of papers was handed to the BDM woman behind the desk. She looked at me with searching eyes. "It has been reported that you have avoided attending the regular Saturday Hitler Youth meetings. For this reason we must tell you that the ration stamps for you and your family will be canceled unless you sign this paper."

With that, she pushed a form toward me. As I looked down, the print blurred in front of my eyes. My thoughts were racing again: "Marga's mother might be able to help out with milk and eggs, but where would we get bread and other food? We have an expectant mother in the family who needs all the nourishment she can get." I took the offered pen and, breathing deeply, signed the paper, which by now I knew to be an application for the Hitler Youth.

The women were pleased and smiled. "You may leave now," one said. "But don't forget to join the group next Saturday." I nodded and left in a daze.

"Hey, come back! Don't you know the German salute?"

I turned around, lifted my right arm, and said what they wanted to hear.

"That's right. And don't you ever forget it!"

I shook my head again as I looked for the exit. Margot was sitting on the front steps, waiting for me. I was still in a state of shock and speechless. Margot however smiled and chatted as if nothing out of the ordinary had happened. There was no more talk about going to her aunt's for a swim. I didn't care now. I just wanted to get home.

While she was chatting away, I wondered why she had never come for me on Saturday afternoons. I would have gone with her, since I knew it was a must for every child to attend the HJ. But that she had done it in this way was awful. I had forgotten all about the meetings after having spent my Saturdays at the theater back in Allenstein. Mutti and Gerda, busy with their own domestic chores, didn't remind me either.

For many years I could not remember how I got home that afternoon or what was said along the way. I was in a daze, caused in part by the deep hurt of Margot's betrayal. It was no use getting angry about it. That would not change what had happened. I only knew that she was no longer a friend of mine and had never really been one. The way she was raised, she probably thought she had done a good deed and me a favor.

"Where have you been so long?" Mutti asked when I entered the kitchen. "You're pale. Aren't you feeling well?"

"I'm all right, Mutti. I think I'm just hungry. Is there any food left?"

"Yes, we left you some potato soup in the pot."

I started to eat, but my stomach was still very tight. I pushed the bowl away. I had to tell Mutti and Gerda what had happened. They both listened attentively. Then Mutti laughed and dismissed the whole matter with a wave of her hand: "What they did is illegal. The signature of a minor is not binding."

Gerda nodded. "Don't get so upset," she said. "It might be fun. Besides, your old friends Marga and Annemie will be there too." I calmed down. They were right. I'd just have to wait and see.

45

The Intruders

The first day of summer vacation felt great. After spending the afternoon swimming and playing in the lake, I came home in time for dinner. Afterwards I curled up in my bed with a book, while Struppy and Murzel, our two dogs, shared the end of the bed with me.

Mutti and Gerda had gone out to meet Ilse Albrecht at the movies. Before leaving, Mutti made sure, as she did every evening, that the windows were properly covered with the thick black blankets. However, I needed only the small lamp on the night table to read by. The other part of our apartment was dark.

An hour must have passed, and I, tired from my afternoon outside in the sun, was about to close my book, turn off the light, and go to sleep when I heard strange whistling sounds. They seemed to be coming from below the windows from two different directions, like signals. Both dogs, instantly on their feet, were making low growling sounds. Then I heard steps coming up the back staircase and stopping at our door. The main entrance downstairs was never locked.

By now both dogs were running through the kitchen towards the corridor and barking wildly. Fortunately, Mutti had left the doors leading to the kitchen and corridor open; otherwise I wouldn't have heard the footsteps. My heart pounding, I got up from the bed and followed the dogs.

"Hello! Is anybody home?" It was a man's voice. "I am the air-raid warden in the neighborhood. I noticed some light leaking out from a corner of a window on the street side of your apartment. I need to inspect and correct it."

I noticed that the man didn't speak with the local accent. Therefore he could not have been our air-raid warden.

"Please open the door," he demanded. Looking to the left, I saw that all the lights in the front rooms were turned off. Something was very wrong here. A shiver went up my spine, but somehow I managed to muster a loud, authoritative voice.

"There are no lights on in the front part of our apartment. Who are you? What's your name?"

No answer. To my horror I saw that the doorknob was being turned from the other side. Still, I knew it was locked. My little dogs had become so furious by this point that they were jumping nearly to the top of the door—up and down, up and down—barking with fury.

`"Don't you dare break in," I screamed. "My two Dobermanns will tear you to pieces if you do!" Someone from the village would have known that we had only two small dogs. Then I heard two voices whispering, although only one had spoken to me. Then I heard the sound of slowly retreating footsteps as they went back downstairs. My dogs continued to bark for a long time after they left.

Pfew! I jumped back into bed and turned on some music to calm me down. The dogs came in and lay down on either side of me, as if to guard me. Going to sleep was out of the question. I would stay up till Mutti and Gerda got back from the show. "Who were those strangers, for heaven's sake?" I weighed the different possibilities. Perhaps they were Party people who wanted to snoop around to see if we were hiding someone or to check Vati's desk. Anyone not adhering to the strict Party line these days was suspected of treason. Why had they asked me those questions about Vati the other day?

Or perhaps the strangers were Russian paratroop spies who spoke fluent German and were looking for food and German clothes. The newspaper had written about such things recently. The whistling sounds which the dogs and I heard at the very beginning had made me suspicious. But what was especially confusing, I realized, was that my own countrymen as well as the Russians had become my enemies now.

Mutti and Gerda got home late because they had stopped at Ilse's place for a snack after the movies. They found me wide awake.

"Child, why aren't you sleeping?" Mutti asked. "It's past midnight."

"Don't ever leave me at home alone at night again," I answered. "Two men came after ten o'clock and tried to open the door. I was so frightened."

Then I told them the whole story. They listened, shaking their heads. Perhaps my imagination had played a trick on me, they thought.

"But what about the dogs?" I asked. "I have never seen them act so wild." I could not believe that my mother and sister had dismissed this incident so lightly. They changed their tune soon thereafter, though, when Marga came over crying one day. She told us that her father had been missing for a week. He had left his garrison by bike on a Saturday morning to go home to supervise the harvest. The family had done everything possible to find him, but all to no avail. How sad and frightening!

46

Whose Side Is God On?

Taking a box filled with old toys to the attic one day—not realizing how useless it was to store them, since my children would never see them—I came upon a half-opened carton which Oma Dorchen had shipped to Vati just before the outbreak of the war. Curious, I found all kinds of World War I memorabilia like antique Russian revolvers, belts, buckles, and buttons from uniforms, all of which Opa Karl must have found along the railway tracks after the Russian Army had been defeated. These items would probably have some value in the future, he must have thought.

There was also a large book in German. It contained photographs of battlefields and marching soldiers. Amazing! There was a Russian unit carrying a large poster picturing Jesus Christ, his hand raised in blessing, into battle. The opposite page showed an enlarged photo of a German soldier whose belt buckle contained the large inscription, *"Gott mit Uns"* ["God with Us"].

For heaven's sakes!" I thought. "Whose side is God supposed to be on?"

Then I remembered watching troops enter the Garrison Church in the old-city part of Allenstein. They were attending a religious service before going off to the front to kill and be killed.

47

Leaving East Prussia

The last days of August were extremely hot. No breeze brought relief. Although we had spent the whole day at the lake, at 7 p.m. I felt ready for another dip in the cool water. Grabbing my bike, I rode down in my bathing suit.

The beach was empty; everyone had gone home for supper. The water looked like a mirror. I climbed the two-meter tower, walked to the end of the board, and dove in head first. Well, not exactly head first. Despite all my recent practice, I performed a perfect belly flop. Ouch! Never mind! I enjoyed the cool water and swam back ready to take on the five-meter tower. This time I had no intention of diving. Instead, I prepared to jump in feet first. When I reached the end of the board, however, I noticed how high up we were and got a little dizzy. Still, closing my eyes, down I went. It wasn't so bad. Surfacing, I decided to do it again.

As I reached the top of the tower this time, I paused and, holding on to the railing, suddenly felt engulfed by an absolute stillness I had never experienced in this place before. A moment later I heard deep humming drifting across the lake from the sandy beach and wooded hill on the other side. In the twilight I could make out a dark group of men, and it was obvious as the humming grew louder and louder that it was coming from them. I soon recognized the melody as the "Russian Evening Bell Song." So I concluded that the men were Russian prisoners of war whom the German guards had brought to the lake to cool off.

How beautiful it sounded, yet at the same time how haunting! Suddenly I had a strange feeling, as if something were happening behind my back. Turning around, I saw a dark wall of clouds rapidly building up on the horizon. Just ahead of the clouds I noticed a spooky yellow-greenish light. Oh my God! I thought. I have to get out of here now.

Wet as I was, I grabbed my bike and took off as fast as I could. Half way home, a terrible wind out of nowhere started bending the trees back and forth on either side of the road. I got so scared that the brief trip seemed to take forever. Branches were falling on the sidewalk to the left and right. The wind held me back.

Finally, I reached the schoolyard. Going in through the back entrance of the house, I threw my bike down in the entryway and ran upstairs. Mutti and Gerda were happy to see me.

"Thank God! You came in just in time!" Mutti said. "The lightning flashes are coming rapidly now, and the thunder follows immediately. That's a sign that we are in the middle of the storm."

The three of us went to the bedroom and huddled close to each other on the bed for protection. The storm got worse and worse until there was a massive impact, after which the lights went out. The power plant had been hit. We could see it burning in the distance through one of the windows. Lightning balls were now rolling down the street. The storm continued through the night as it went back and forth among the lakes in our area. We had never seen such a storm. Needless to say, none of us slept that night. I saw Gerda crying as she tried to protect her belly with both her hands. Mutti and I moved in closer to her.

The storm with its furious dark clouds full of electricity had come from the east. It had passed over the battlefields until it reached East Prussia. This was not a good omen. Then I heard the deep humming again inside my head.

The weather suddenly turned cooler, and with September, school resumed. For some reason Fraeulein Schneider II was quite friendly to me now. Soon I found out why. As the highest-ranked **BDM** leader in our district, she of course would know that I was now enrolled in the Kiefernberg unit.

At one of the Saturday meetings, the leader asked me what I could contribute to the group. I told her that I could play theater games with the girls and that I even had a script all ready to go. She laughed but agreed. "All right," she said. "Let's try something new. It's been raining a lot these days, and we have to stay indoors anyway."

My friends got the best parts. Marga was the king, Annemie the princess, and Liselotte, a former classmate, the prince. The other girls made up the court. I of course was once again the court jester.

Some funny things happened. For example, whenever Marga (the king) spoke, I played with her words and gave them different (often silly) meanings. She got angry until she understood that I was doing all this on purpose to make the audience laugh.

"If it hurts your feelings, Marga," I said, "someone else can take your part."

"It's all right," she answered. "I'll be fine. I'll get used to it."

We also had great fun putting together costumes, with borrowed clothes from our brothers and sisters. Anyway, when the big day came, the classroom was full. We had invited our families as well as the children in the neighborhood. To our surprise, even Principal Pipgorra showed up and sat in the last row.

Everything went as planned with the exception of two courtiers who for some unknown reason were trying to kick each other off the stage and the fact that Marga forgot some of her lines. Fortunately, as court jester I could feed them to her. In fact, the audience thought that was part of the show and laughed. A dumb king for most people, it seems, is funny.

From the back row we could hear Pip's deep belly laugh, and with a quick glance I could see that he had almost lost control of his upper bridge again as he had some years before in class, though this time for a more pleasant reason.

It was the last time I would have fun together with my childhood friends.

Weeks went by. Suddenly horse-drawn refugee carts began passing through our village. They were going west. Nearly every night Mutti and I had disturbing dreams. One night when I looked over to Gerda's bed, I saw she had pulled her down comforter up over her head. Muffled sounds were coming from her direction.

"Gerda," I whispered. "What are you doing under there?"

She beckoned me over. Kneeling beside her bed, I could hear the low voice of a radio announcer coming from Gerda's little radio, now under the covers.

"It's the BBC, London," Gerda said.

191

"Are you crazy?" I whispered back. "You know it's forbidden!"

"Nobody can hear this except us," she replied. "I want to know where the Russian Army really is," she continued. "The reports we get from our side must be wrong. Otherwise we would not see so many refugees. According to the BBC, the Russians have already crossed the East Prussian border in the north and are nearing the city of Memel. We have to tell Mutti first thing in the morning so we can begin preparations to leave. I don't want to end up giving birth in a farm wagon. Besides, Annemarie Thiel wrote that if necessary we could go to Striegau, where she is, and she would find us a place to stay. After all, the baby in my belly is her first grandchild."

I nodded. Gerda was totally right to think about finding protection for herself and the unborn child.

"Gerda, why don't we go straightaway to the Howes' in Munich?" I asked.

"Haven't you heard about the recent massive bombings there?" She countered. "Striegau seems a safe enough little town right now. After all, the Government recently relocated the Imperial Patent Office there from Berlin, you know."

"All right, but let's talk to Mutti in the morning."

"That's fine. Now go back to bed, Lore. It's past midnight."

I did but couldn't fall asleep right away. My thoughts darted here and there, and in my heart I felt a deep sadness.

Mutti was not surprised the next morning when we reported what we had heard on the German-language BBC transmission the night before. Over breakfast we discussed what to do.

"Well," Mutti concluded, "our troops may push the Russians back, but for how long? It's better to act while there's still time. I agree with you."

She immediately began sorting out closets and packing up our best clothes, linens, silverware, and other useful items. Our down comforters were put into the big wicker laundry basket, where Mutti also placed our delicate China tea service in the middle for protection. On top of the basket, she tied on a small, square Persian rug before binding everything up with twine.

We brought the big suitcases down from the attic and opened them on the floor. It was so sad to see Struppy and Murtzel, our two lap dogs, jump in and look up at us with sad eyes, as if suspecting the worst. They seemed to be saying, "Take us with you. We don't want to be left behind." It was hard not to cry. We knew it would be impossible to take them with us under the circumstances. The trains would be overcrowded, and food would be scarce. Besides, who would give us a room in Striegau with our two pets?

When Vati took Murtzel—the older, quieter dog—to Uncle Erich's apartment in Allenstein on the weekend, Gerda and I broke down and cried. At least it consoled us to know he was in good hands. On seeing his companion leaving, Struppy jumped at the closed door and barked sadly. We tried to divert his attention by placing a lump of sugar—something he'd always enjoyed—in front of him on the floor. This time he simply ignored it. Instead, he put his face on his front paws and gave us a look as if to say, "I can't be bribed about this." When Mutti told us the following week that she had found a good home for him with a friendly farm family, I threw myself down on my bed and cried for a long time. The parting was heart-breaking. My true little friends who had protected me in an hour of danger were now gone. I knew beyond a doubt that I would never see them again.

We were almost finished packing when the mayor's office told us to make room for some refugees, a woman with two daughters. The beds from Frau Annemarie's room upstairs were installed downstairs in our children's room. We three moved into the master bedroom for our remaining days. As it happened the family came the day before we left. They shared horror stories from their wagon mates who had just escaped being massacred by the Red Army in a neighboring village.

"Frau Zimmermann," the woman gasped, "they said that Russian tanks just drove through houses and barns, ran over animals, and even crushed horse carts with people in them. Whatever women they caught were raped and brutally murdered. It's unimaginable. My husband, who's a colonel in the infantry, saw the destruction for himself when his unit retook some territory. He said he'd never seen anything so horrible. He urged us in a message to leave as quickly as possible."

"We don't know how long it will be safe here," Mutti replied. "That's why I am leaving shortly with my pregnant daughter. Meanwhile, make yourself comfortable in our home and get some rest. You'll need it when you continue your journey west."

The woman nodded sadly.

Mutti had found a friendly old farmer who drove our big basket and fourteen other heavy boxes and suitcases to the railway station for shipment to Striegau. Now came the time for final goodbyes. I had told the girls at our BDM gathering the Saturday before that we would be leaving soon. Nonetheless, I rushed over to Annemie's house to bid her goodbye again and to give her a secret warning. "Please tell your mother to leave in good time, before the Russians reach the outskirts of our town. It may happen sooner than you think."

"I will, Lorchen," she said, squeezing my hand for the last time.

I skipped down the few steps to the street and took a last look at her red-brick house with the white window frames and the old cherry tree in the front. I had eaten a lot of tart cherries this summer from another cherry tree that grew behind the fence around the principal's garden. Often I would climb to the top to pick the ripest cherries. Beneath it we had planted a little vegetable garden that reached into the field. We had harvested a good amount of cucumbers, tomatoes, onions, and lettuce there this year. Now only the sunflowers were left to feed the birds in winter.

Entering the house, I looked around one last time in the children's room, our guests being away in the village. I paged through the books in my bookshelves with all the beautifully illustrated fairy-tale volumes I had collected over the years together with other youth literature. Nobody would read these books after we left, I thought. The soldiers or other new residents would probably use them to fuel the ovens for lack of firewood.

Next I went over to my favorite dolls—Ursel, Karin, and Baerbel—sitting in the little blue stroller which had brought me so much joy on that Christmas Eve long ago. Out of a drawer I pulled some of their woolen doll's clothes with which I dressed them to keep them warm during the coming winter. Tears rolled down my cheeks. "I just hope that in future you will make some other kids happy whoever they might be." Then, getting up abruptly,

I left the room. Closing the door behind me, I took leave of my childhood for good.

In the late afternoon, suitcases in hand, we walked up the street toward the train station. Our plan was to spend two days with the family in Allenstein before moving southwest. When we got to the top of the hill, we turned and looked back at the schoolhouse one last time. There it was, surrounded by old-growth trees now in their full autumn splendor. The colorful leaves glowed intensely in the late-afternoon sun as if they, together with the heavy-headed sunflowers moving slightly in the breeze, wanted to give us a special send-off. It was a picture I photographed in my mind forever.

"We shall never live here again!" Mutti whispered, fighting a lump in her throat. "Come on, girls. Let's go." When we arrived in Allenstein, Oma Dorchen had prepared a light meal for us. We sat around the old dining table talking as we had done during all the years we lived here. Then Vati suddenly shook his head. "I can't believe that Hitler has ordered our crack East Prussian divisions to the Western Front. They are needed much more here. He obviously has a very low regard for the Red Army. He even had the nerve to call the soldiers sub humans. Apparently he is more afraid of the Americans. It's idiotic and a shame that his generals don't tell him the truth. Yet we must not lose hope but simply prepare ourselves for the worst.

"So be on guard, Trude, and if the front starts closing in on Silesia, make sure you leave in enough time. Remember, you have a place in a suburb of Munich waiting for you. We all have the address so we can join you after the war. I gave it to your parents, Heinz, and Erich as well."

Heinz, her officer-husband, came to pick up Gerda

and take her to the hotel for the night. I slept on the couch in Oma's room. However, I had a hard time falling asleep, and so did Oma Dorchen. I heard her coughing as she tossed and turned. Sensing that I was still awake, she suddenly spoke to me: "Lorchen, remember what I am about to tell you. When I die, please ask your father or mother to put the white statue of the welcoming Jesus into my coffin with me. It was a wedding gift, and I've kept it all these years on the shelf above my bed. I'm sure you've noticed."

"Yes, Oma."

"Well, since one of the arms broke off during a move," she continued, "it has only sentimental value now. Nobody would want it. So, don't forget to tell them my wishes when the time comes."

"I won't, Oma."

I had a strange feeling. Did Oma have a premonition that she would die soon? Why did she choose to tell me, a child, her last wish? Perhaps she figured the other family members were too preoccupied with their own problems and that I as a youngster had a better memory. The conversation, however, did nothing to help me fall asleep.*

---

*This problem was taken care of by Russian planes which destroyed Oma's entire block on the Hermann Goering Strasse with their bombs. Not only that, but the planes took out the railway bridge the day after Oma and her sons had left town in January 1945—just as I had foreseen from the roof of Oma's apartment house in 1943.

197

48

Christmas and
New Year's Eve, 1944

The week before Christmas the sky was overcast, and a cold drizzle fell. As in Osterode two months earlier, the first refugees with their overloaded farm wagons now slowly began to push their way into town from the receding Eastern Front.

The last days before vacation thus lacked the usual joyful anticipation for us school children. In fact, the atmosphere in the classroom was as oppressive as the weather. Despite the continuing positive military bulletins on the radio, people paid less and less heed. We kids began to wonder what would happen to us and our families in the months ahead.

Fortunately, the mood changed immediately when our favorite teacher, Dr. Waechter, entered the classroom with a smile to teach us Greek history. He was a tall, slender gentleman in his 70's, almost bald with a little gray mustache and kindly blue eyes. Seating himself on the table in the empty front row, he said, "Well, my young friends, we shall forget about our studies today. So, please put your books away. Instead, we'll have story time."

With that, he began to talk about his youth, during the days when he had traveled through Greece. His descriptions of all the places of antiquity he had visited were so colorful and vivid that we sat glued to our seats and could not hear enough. For an hour he took us out of the gloomy reality of Germany at war and transported us to the sunny, silvery world of ancient Hellas.

"Now remember," he encouraged us; "you too will be able to see all this for yourselves someday if you study hard and establish yourselves in the world."

The seeds of hope this man was trying to plant in our hearts were an incredible blessing. Even though we had him for only a short time, I have never forgotten this inspired and inspiring teacher.

Heinz, Gerda's husband, got a seven-day pass from the Army around December 10th. He would have to be back at his office before the Holidays to give his comrades a chance to visit their larger families for Christmas. He brought with him a Holiday package from Vati. It contained canned goods, two large salamis, home-baked cookies from Oma Dorchen, a few packs of cigarettes for Mutti, and a bottle of Cognac. Heinz and Gerda had to stay in a small pension [bed-and-breakfast], because neither Heinz's parents nor we had enough space to put them up. As it happened, it would be the last time they would be together for the next two-and-a-half years.

Mutti, Gerda, and I spent Christmas alone. For atmosphere we had a little tree on the night table between our two beds. Somehow against all odds, Mutti had managed to find presents for us—though we had no idea how she had done it. Out of a white box she handed each of us a dark-blue taffeta dress with a large white embroidered collar. The labels indicated they had come from a boutique in Vienna.

The unexpected gifts cheered us up for a while. Soon, though, we became quiet, as each of us followed our own thoughts. It was the first time the family had not been together for Christmas, and we each felt a bit forlorn and lost "under" our little tree in this strange, if still German place. Vati must miss us too, I thought, but at least he would be spending this sacred evening with his mother and Uncle Erich back in Allenstein. Tante Elly had left by train the end of November to stay with her brother's wife in the town of Eisleben in Thuringia. There, well away from the Front, she gave birth on December 18th to my new cousin, Gisela, as Vati had reported in his last letter.

Having no radio, we missed the traditional Christmas Eve music program. Since the growing cold outside had changed the rain-slicked streets into sheets of ice, it was too dangerous to walk in the dark to church, especially for our expectant mother. When our attempts to sing carols ourselves fizzled, we decided to turn in early. Besides, the room temperature had dropped to an uncomfortable degree. Fortunately, I shared the bed with Mutti, so we could warm each other against the cold.

On Christmas morning the sun came back and melted the ice to slush by the time we had to meet Gerda's in-laws in town. Frau Annemarie had learned that a restaurant on a hilltop outside town was offering a Christmas lunch, so we decided to go there. We enjoyed the little walk through a wooded area to the restaurant. From a safe distance behind fences, deer inspected us intruders with their dark eyes. Gerda, wearing flat, comfortable shoes, did well climbing the hilly path considering she was in her seventh month. We were looking forward to a warm meal. The only one offered— Surprise! Surprise!—proved to be venison. No wonder the deer near the restaurant had been enclosed. Poor deer!

We chose a table next to the window for its beautiful view of the town below. Christmas music was playing. Finally, some Holiday cheer! Suddenly, in the middle of our meal, strange noises interrupted the music. All at once a husky male voice with a Russian accent came through: "You German pigs, while you are stuffing yourselves with *Gaensebraten* [roasted goose], listen to my words. Your days of victory are over. Just wait to see what we will do to you when we come. No pleading or screaming will help you. We will smash all of you to pieces. Just wait and see!" Then the voice faded back into the noise, and the Christmas music took over again.

We had stopped eating and dumbly stared at each other, unable to say a word. What we had heard was nothing new. It simply confirmed the stories of the refugees passing through town. The sunshine seemed to have disappeared behind a dark cloud, leaving oppressive shadows hanging over the room. Walking home, Gerda took a few snapshots with her box camera. However, none of us felt like talking. Even the usually voluble Frau Annemarie kept silent.

For Silvester [New Year's Eve], I was invited to dinner by my host family and to spend the evening with my roommate, Ingrid. At midnight we gathered in the living room to greet the New Year. But mainly we feared for the future. Our mood was not helped by a fierce pep talk to the Volk given on the radio by Dr. Goebbels, Hitler's propaganda minister. If the German people did not live up to the Fuehrer's expectation that we would defend the Vaterland by all means available, even our fists, he said, then the future would be dark indeed. Considering all that our SS troops had reportedly done in the countries to our East, he had the impertinence to call President Roosevelt the greatest war criminal of all time. Our hosts shook their heads. In their eyes there was not the faintest glimmer of hope.

That night I dreamed I was back in our old village.

However, when I tried to walk toward our home in the school building, my feet sunk into the soft ground, and I could go no farther. Telling this dream to Mutti the next day, I said, "There's no way we'll be able to go back again." Looking at me with a grave expression, she nodded in agreement.

49

Escape from Silesia

School in Striegau [Silesia] began as usual after Epiphany on January 6 but continued only for a week or so. The reason was that the classrooms had become dormitories for exhausted refugee families arriving in ever greater numbers from the east.

One day Mutti took us over to Gerda's in-laws. She told them it was high time, in her opinion, for us to leave Striegau for the Munich suburb of Gruenwald, where we could stay with Hans Howe's family.

"Besides Gerda's condition," she said, "I am not confident that the radio reports on the whereabouts of the Russian Army are accurate. Recently I asked a local official about the thunder-like noises coming from the east. He assured me that it was only our army detonating charges to break up the ice on the Oder. Somehow I don't believe that's all it is.

"Also, I had a vivid dream last night in which the entire population of Striegau was commanded to line up in the market square. There, women commissars separated them into groups of men, women, and children who were then loaded onto separate trucks and driven off. I consider this dream a warning not to stay here any longer."

Agreeing, both Thiels said we should follow our gut feelings. When Mutti talked with my hosts about her idea, they said they also had plans to leave. They mentioned they had friends who owned a big farm outside Dresden, where they were sending their furniture in a large truck. We were welcome to join in with our things if we wished. This seemed like a good opportunity, since our big boxes were still unpacked in a storage facility, and this arrangement would save us time.

After Mutti agreed and got everything set up, we went to the post office to try to reach Vati by telephone in his office. The date was January 19, 1945. It took a long time to get through, but she finally succeeded. She wanted to tell him we would be leaving Striegau the next day for Munich so he would know where to look for us later.

Back home, we packed our few belongings in three suitcases. The smallest, filled mainly with diapers, baby clothes, and a maternity dress, I would carry. Gerda was in charge of the leather briefcase containing family documents and other papers. She also carried the big bag with food for the trip. Mutti had managed to organize a whole salami, a loaf of bread, a thermos filled with tea, and a bottle of cognac left over from Christmas. The last packs of cigarettes were stuffed into the corners. Fruit had not been available for a long time, so of course we had none of that. Before Mutti closed the suitcases, I made sure the family photo albums I had rescued in Kiefernberg were again put on top.

We went to sleep early that night so we could leave when it was still dark. The in-laws had come to the station to see us off, but it was a hard struggle to get into the overcrowded train with our luggage. Besides, we had to protect Gerda on both sides from pushing people. Mutti and I stood halfway on the wobbly metal bridge connecting two train cars. Gerda was finally safely inside, thank God.

Puffing clouds of white steam into the ice-cold air, our engine finally managed to pull its heavy load forward. As we slowly moved out of the station, we waved goodbyes to the two faces fading into the mist of the platform. We did not know if we would ever see the elder Thiels again.

After approximately 50 minutes, we arrived in the city of Liegnitz, where we had to change trains for Dresden. If it had been difficult to find room in the train from Striegau to Liegnitz, the situation here looked hopeless. Seeing overloaded trains all around us, we began to despair. What should we do? An icy wind was blowing from the east. It was so cold; we felt our toes getting numb.

"Wait for me here," Mutti told us. "I'll be right back!" Following her with my eyes, I saw her approaching a Red Cross train in the distance. Soon she was talking and gesturing to a man in a long, gray coat.

Smiling with relief, she ran up to us. "Come, follow me quickly," she gasped as she grabbed the two larger suitcases. I walked with Gerda who was moving as fast as she could. She looked pale. "Oh, God! Does she need rest!" I thought.

Mutti had stopped in front of an open door to a 3rd-class car. A young, blond physician appeared together with a nurse in the traditional white Red Cross uniform. Smiling, they motioned to us to climb in. It was the sort of train car farmers used to bring their produce to market. Wooden benches were placed along the walls, with a big empty space left in the middle. By the time we got there, every seat was taken, mainly by old people who had been evacuated from a nursing home. A wounded soldier was sitting with his wife in one corner. Someone had brought a sled along. It was placed in the middle of the car and topped with several down comforters.

"Would you mind letting this pregnant woman use the sled as a bed?" The doctor asked the couple. "As you can see, she really needs to lie down."

"We would be happy to," the couple responded.

For a while I sat on my suitcase. However, it had to be stacked away since it was blocking the small path to the next car, a freight car covered with straw for wounded soldiers and very sick people. I looked around and felt relieved when I saw the sign WC indicating a private toilet at the end of the car.

"How did you manage to get us in?" I whispered to Mutti, who was sitting on the edge of a bench in front of me while I was leaning on the closed, covered window next to some other people who had no seats.

"Well, I started by pleading for Gerda. When the doctor saw the Red Cross pin on my coat, he said, 'I need your help. I have only one nurse for the whole train. We can't do everything. Besides, your pregnant daughter has every right to be here.'"

Mutti had just finished her explanation when the door was thrust open and two big members of the *Feldgendarmerie* [German MPs] walked in. They were checking papers.

"What are these two doing here?" One of them asked, pointing at Mutti and me.

The doctor stepped forward and explained that Mutti was a trained Red Cross volunteer. "I need her very badly since I have only one nurse for the whole train!"

They nodded, then turned to me. "What about her? She is young and has good legs. She can walk."

With that they grabbed me and were about to throw me off the train. It all happened so fast. I simply stared at Mutti, helpless.

"Wait a minute!" I heard the doctor's voice. "You

can't separate them. She's this woman's child. Don't you dare! Otherwise, I'll leave the train myself, and then there'll be no physician on board, you understand?"

He had spoken with a calm, authoritative voice. The two MPs let me go, backed out, and left. All the other people in the car seemed to have held their breath during the brief encounter, since now I heard a collective sigh of relief. Mutti put her arms around me and, tears in her eyes, thanked the brave man for the risk he had taken to save me. I was still in shock. Holding Mutti's hand, I sat down on the floor.

We were wrong, however, to think our ordeal was over. Some minutes later the nurse came in from outside and, clearly agitated, reported that some city officials had taken our locomotive for their own private train and that there were no others left in the station. Meanwhile, the Russians were nearing the far end of the city. Already some residential blocks were burning from Russian artillery shells. The situation had gone from bad to worse. We stared at each other in despair. Suddenly I heard murmuring from a group of elderly women in the back of the car. What were they saying? As it got louder, I realized they were intoning the same prayer over and over in unison:

> *Heilige Maria, voller Gnaden,*
> *Der Herr ist mit Dir.*
> *Du bist gebenedeit unter den Weibern*
> *Und gebenedeit ist die Frucht Deines Leibes*
> *Jesus.*
> *Heilige Maria, Mutter Gottes,*
> *Bitt fuer uns jetzt*
> *Und in der Stunde unseres Todes.*
> *Amen!*

Hail, Mary, full of Grace,
The Lord is with Thee.
Blessed art Thou among women
And blessed is the fruit of Thy womb
Jesus.
Holy Mary, Mother of God,
Pray for us sinners now
And at the hour of our death,
Amen.

"Mutti, what time is it?" I asked.

"Two in the afternoon," she answered and sighed.

Would we all die here, or would a miracle save us? Perhaps I don't deserve to be saved after all the naughty things I've done, I reflected, especially given my recent denial of God. Would he ever listen to me again if I prayed? I wondered. A wave of anger welled up in me. "God, you are supposed to be almighty. If that is so, why do you let all these wars, disasters, plagues, and periods of starvation happen?"

Calmness soon filled my chest, and I became aware of a voice, not mine, talking inside me. "Lift the window curtain," it said. I did. What I saw was a multitude of women and children crying to be let in, slapping their arms in the cold in an attempt to stay warm. And then the voice continued, "God does not want these things to happen. What you see is the result of people doing wrong things. God does not interfere because he gave human beings free will."

Then it struck me like lightning. If human beings turn to God in utmost sincerity and ask for help, miracles could happen. Yes. That was it. Only a miracle could save us now.

"Oh God," I prayed. "You may not look with favor on me, but what about Gerda's unborn baby? It has not done anything bad. For his sake, please have mercy!"

Then I joined the others in saying the Rosary with all my heart and strength. Soon I fell into a kind of rhythm. After a while I remembered the Lord's Prayer and others Mutti had taught me years ago. Then, leaning against the wall and looking up, I whispered with great intensity, "God, it is said you can move mountains. If so, I believe that you can move this train too!"

With that, still leaning against the wall, I fell into a deep sleep. Suddenly I was jerked forward and opened my eyes. It was dark, but I could definitely feel the wheels under my feet turning. The train was moving!

"Mutti, can you see your watch? What time is it?"

"I just asked the doctor. He has a flashlight." Mutti replied. "It's half past nine. He went to see if he could find someone to fix the lights. Try to sleep till Goerlitz, our next stop. There should be someone there who can restore our electricity."

But no one, including me, felt like sleeping. We were all so overjoyed and excited that our prayers had been answered and that the train was now rolling. We were also hungry, but how could we find our bag with food in the dark?

The doctor had just returned. He suggested we take down the black-out paper from the windows. It was snowing outside, and the snow-covered fields, he thought, would reflect enough light for us to eat by.

Mutti reached for our provision bag. She cut thin slices of bread and small pieces of salami so that there was enough for everyone. Others had hard-boiled eggs or cakes, which they also shared around. It was like a party to celebrate our miraculous escape.

Mutti next held up the bottle of cognac. "Herr Doktor, take a sip to warm your stomach. Please do it for all of us. You deserve it the most."

He laughed and did as he was told.

Mutti had another idea. "Herr Doktor, since there isn't much disinfectant left, maybe we could use the cognac with boiled water to make a solution to wash the soldiers' wounds later on."

"Well, we'll have to melt snow tomorrow morning and boil it in the kettle in the next car, since we have only a little drinking water left for the wounded."

Mutti and the nurse nodded their agreement.

I turned to them and asked how the train had been able to leave Liegnitz. The nurse responded: "As it happened, there were four retired railroad engineers among the sick on our train. When they heard our situation, they scouted around the station until they found a partially damaged engine at the far end. Refusing to despair, even though they all had been recovering from various illnesses in the Breslau Hospital, they believed they could fix the problem. Finding the repair building, they were able to locate the tools and spare parts they needed. In a relatively short time they were able to put together a working engine and even shovel in a load of coal. It's a real miracle. Unbelievable!" We all applauded.

Our good old engine, fragile as it was, broke down several times on the way to Goerlitz, but the main thing was that each kilometer we traveled took us farther away from the Front. In later years I often reflected on what this incident had to say about miracles in general. Many people have the idea that miracles always have to be supernatural and the beneficial changes instantaneous. In our case, what happened occurred in a natural way and took a number of hours. Nonetheless, those four old men, as frail and sick as they were, had been inspired by the Grace of God to seek a solution, find what they needed, and have the strength, hope, and determination to get the job done before the Russians arrived. A miracle indeed!

Finally, fatigue overtook us, and we all managed to sleep in whatever position we found ourselves. In the middle of the night I was awakened by some commotion in my vicinity. Mutti, the doctor, and the nurse were whispering. Apparently a woman, already the mother of five children, was going into labor two cars ahead of us.

"Of course I can help," I heard Mutti say. "When I was living in the country, I assisted several times. Do you have any clean sheets or towels?"

"No. I'm afraid all we have left are sterile bandage material and some blankets," the nurse answered.

"Let's hurry!" The doctor broke in. "We just have to put her on a new blanket in a makeshift bed on straw. When the train stops again, Frau Zimmermann, you can get a bucket full of snow for boiling. It will still take a while for the baby to come out."

When they left, I moved to Mutti's seat, leaned back, and fell asleep again. When I woke up, I had to squint from the strong reflection of sunlight off the snow. Gerda was still fast asleep on her comforter-bedecked sled. Thank Goodness for that!

Mutti, looking exhausted, re-entered our car. I gave her her seat back. "When did the baby arrive?" I asked. "It looks like you haven't slept at all."

"No, I haven't," Mutti whispered in my ear. She didn't want to wake Gerda nor have her hear what had happened. "The woman was very weak to begin with," Mutti continued, "but she put up a great struggle for several hours until, with help from the doctor and the nurse, the baby was pushed out. All our efforts were in vain, however, because the child was stillborn."

"You mean it was not alive, Mutti?"

"Yes. That's the expression used, stillborn.

"How is the mother doing?" I wanted to know.

Mutti only shook her head and gave me a sad look: "She'd lost a lot of blood, Lorchen, and had no more strength. Two hours later she was gone too. Before she died, she begged us to take care of her five children. An elderly woman who had stayed in the compartment with us the whole time, walked over to the woman, took her hand, and said, 'I'm going home to the Rhineland, where I own a large winery. I'll take the children with me—we have plenty of room there—and I'll also look for the father.' The mother gave her a faint smile, closed her eyes, and died."

Mutti wiped the tears from her cheeks. I glanced over at Gerda. "Oh God," I prayed. "Please protect her and the baby until we arrive at our destination."

A little while later, the train stopped again. Sitting on my suitcase, I was able to look out the window. There was not much to see except for a few barren trees and some bushes dotting the flat landscape. Then I saw the doctor and the nurse carrying a bundle out of one of the cars and placing it next to a big stone with a number on it. I called Mutti over. "What are they doing?" I asked.

"Ach!" She sighed. "They can't leave dead bodies on the train any longer, since nobody knows when we'll get

212

to Goerlitz with our engine. It may take another day. So they are placing the bodies with some identification papers next to the railway milestone. Once we get to Goerlitz, the doctor will notify the police in the village closest to where they left the bodies."

I turned away from the window. "How awful, Mutti! I hope the children don't see this."

"No, no. They are still asleep, and we made sure the windows were covered."

Gerda woke up. "Is there some tea in the thermos?" She asked

"Of course, and you can have something to eat too," Mutti replied, reaching for the bread and the salami.

I ate my slice of bread now too. As hungry as I was, it tasted almost like cake.

Our engine did the best it could. We nevertheless had several more stops during the day while the four old men worked hard so that the locomotive could again function. It was not so cold anymore with the sun now shining. Those who could, got out and walked. We washed our hands and faces in the fresh snow and felt a little refreshed. I even rinsed my mouth with some snow. We also collected it to be boiled for drinking water for the rest of the day and the night we'd have to spend on board.

Mutti and the nurse were busy all day long taking care of the wounded with the remaining supply of bandages and dressings. The last of the aspirins were given to the sick and wounded who had fever. In the late afternoon, our three-person medical team came back to our car for a rest. By nightfall the train was moving again. Mutti shared the rest of the bread and salami with our fellow passengers. She only made sure to keep some back for Gerda's

213

breakfast. The nurse had some black tea which she placed in an aluminum container with the boiling snow water. Everybody was happy to get something warm into their stomachs. Several old people had brought along their personal drinking mugs. These were filled with tea and passed around so that everyone could get a sip or two.

Today people felt relaxed enough to start talking with each other. I overheard the doctor tell Mutti, "I was born Dutch and began my medical studies in Holland. I must confess that I never completed them. After my fourth semester, the German occupation forces in my country ordered me to join a Red Cross ambulance unit. I am nevertheless grateful that I can be of service in these chaotic circumstances and help people with what training I have."

"Well, words are not enough to thank you for what you did for the girls and me," Mutti said. "I can't even imagine what would have happened to us in Liegnitz if you had not allowed us to join your train."

Gerda, who was now sitting up in her makeshift bed, nodded and added her thanks as well. I just stared at him and remembered how he had stood up for me, most likely saving my life. My eyes filled with tears.

"Schon gut, schon gut, kleines Fraeulein!" ["Forget about it, little miss!"], he laughed. "We didn't want to lose you, now did we?" I smiled back. He was our hero.

As exhausted as we were, we slept longer this night. By 11 a.m. the next morning our train finally pulled into the Goerlitz station. We were surprised to see groups of Hitler Youth and BDM there to greet us. Behind them we noticed a big, steaming kettle on a table with aluminum bowls. "You must be very hungry," they shouted. "Come have some soup!" They didn't have to ask twice. We all hurried to the table and grabbed a bowl. Then I noticed that the doctor and the nurse, laughing, had gotten into a snowball fight. Obviously they were pleased to have brought their valuable (and vulnerable) cargo to safety.

We stayed in Goerlitz for a few hours, since our doctor had demanded, and had gotten, a new engine.

"How on earth were you able to get this thing to move?" One of the railroad inspectors asked after having taken a look at our strung-together collection of parts. "It just did somehow," the doctor explained.

We made use of the relatively clean restroom at the station. The fresh water and soap helped us revive a little. Gerda had packed her box camera in the food bag at the last minute before we left for the train in Striegau. She now took some pictures outside our train car of the doctor and the nurse, and they took one of us. During the last few years Gerda had emerged as the official family photographer. She was quite good at it, actually. Alas, only a few of her pictures survived the war.

From the noise our train was now making, it was obvious that, thanks to the new engine, we were moving at a decent clip. Sitting on my suitcase, I watched the white landscape glide by. Everything looked so peaceful.

All at once our train came to a halt. We were on the crest of a high hill. We guessed that we had stopped to let another train pass. On the other side of the car, Gerda, who was standing by the window, motioned for us to come over. Far below and still at a considerable distance, the city lay before us, its buildings, windows, and steeples gilded by the afternoon sun. Gerda and Heinz had been here last year on their honeymoon. She looked down for a long time, absorbed in her thoughts. Suddenly she moaned and touched her side. Mutti rushed over to help her return to her sled. Mutti apparently knew where the pain was coming from and called the doctor. She looked concerned, but he tried to play it down by saying Gerda was most likely having false labor.

"Soon we'll be in Dresden," he said. "Try to get her immediate medical attention there. For now, just let her rest."

Mutti and I sat quietly together. We were both praying silently to get the help we once again needed.

50

A Fateful Stop in Dresden

It was dark when we finally arrived. We needed to leave our train here and find one going to Munich. There was no time to give our two rescuers more than brief goodbyes and thank-yous. We had no idea what our next steps would be, since we'd heard that the last train to South Germany had already left.

Keeping a watchful eye on Gerda, we made our way slowly into the great station hall. A dreadful scene greeted us. Every inch of floor was covered with people sitting or lying, wounded soldiers on stretchers moaning, and babies crying. The air was filled with the smell of urine and smoke. There was barely room to stand. Gerda, pressing her lips together, leaned on Mutti's shoulder.

All of a sudden out of nowhere a small figure in a trench coat and beige rain hat, stepping over luggage and around people, approached us. Standing in front of us now and giving us each a concerned look, she said, "I come here every evening and take people home who seem to need help." Then pointing to Gerda, she continued, "I see this young woman needs it most of all. How are you doing, little mother?"

"Not too well," Gerda responded. "For some time now I've been having pains. Oh, and this is my mother and my sister Lore."

The woman gave us a friendly nod and said, "Now, come along with me, all of you."

Outside the station, the fresh air did us good. It was pitch dark, and while Mutti and I carried the luggage, the little lady took Gerda's arm and guided her carefully along the blacked-out street. Soon we found ourselves in front of a large building. The high front door resembled a heavy gate. After it swung open, our hostess motioned us to follow her quickly. Some light was shimmering through a curtain from inside and threatened to violate the blackout.

The iron door closed behind us with a bang. When the curtain was pushed aside, we entered a long corridor flooded with bright light. Large paintings in golden frames lined the walls. We could not believe our eyes. It was as if we had awakened in a dream world.

Our hostess opened a door on the right. "This is your room for the night. Please make yourselves comfortable. I'll go call a doctor."

"Thank you so much," Mutti replied, turning down the covers on a large bed in the middle of the room. The bed was so big that the three of us could fit, even taking into account Gerda's belly. All I can remember is kicking off my shoes and plunging into the soft, white down comforter, which felt like heaven.

I don't know how long we had slept when energetic knocking woke us up. "Who is it?" Mutti said, turning on the little night-table lamp and going to the door.

"Please open the door. I've found a doctor to examine your daughter."

A tall man in a white coat entered the room and greeted us. "Please tell your younger daughter to go out for a little while. You may remain here while I take a look at your older daughter."

"Mutti, what time is it?" I asked.

"Four a.m.," she replied, helping me out of bed.

I wondered how the little lady had gotten a doctor to come out in the middle of the night to help total strangers. I stumbled into a small room across the hall, where I fell into a large armchair. How I got back to our room remains a mystery. When I next awoke, sunlight was shining on my face. Gerda was sitting up in bed while Mutti was opening suitcases in search of clean underwear.

"Go wash up now," she instructed me. The bathroom is two doors down on the left. There's even warm water."

By the time I got back it was already 11 o'clock. "What did the doctor say, Mutti?" I asked.

"He said Gerda was having false labor brought on by the extreme hardship of our trip. He gave her an injection and advised her to rest as much as she could. However, he also urged us to leave the city as soon as possible. He refused to accept any payment. He'd just stopped by on his way to the railroad station, he said, where he was going to attend to the wounded. What a gentleman! Wishing us a good trip to Munich, he left as quickly as he had come. By the way, our hostess gave me directions to a restaurant nearby where they serve decent food. So, let's go, girls. Aren't you hungry?"

"Of course, Mutti," we replied together.

Grabbing our coats and gloves, we walked out the front door. Gerda said she had no pain now and was glad to have the chance to stretch her legs. The large restaurant was only a short walk. It was crowded and smelled of stale beer. Cigarette smoke hung in the air like fog due to the inadequate ventilation. It was also noisy. Luckily we found a table. Mutti pulled out some ration coupons so we could order soup and sauerbraten (marinated roast beef) with potatoes. When the food came, we wolfed it down. How delicious it tasted! Still, we were eager to leave the pollution of the place as soon as we could.

On the way back to the big house, we stopped by a store to buy some rolls and a vegetarian spread, since neither cheese nor cold cuts were available. Gerda had to lie down as soon as we arrived, while Mutti left for the railroad station to check on the possibility of getting a train to Bavaria that night. It took some time for her to return. The platforms, she reported, were as flooded with people as those at Liegnitz had been. "I'm sure it won't be any better tomorrow and may even be worse, since refugees like us keep arriving each day. So we'll just have to try tonight and hope for the best. May God help us once again!"

Mutti had managed to buy some peppermint tea and vitamin C tablets at the drugstore on the way back. We stretched out and slept till around 6 p.m. The rolls with brewed peppermint tea became our supper. The remaining tea was poured into the thermos for the trip.

Just as we were dressed and prepared to leave for the station, the air was violated by the frightening sound of the air-raid warning. We looked around the hall for a door leading to a shelter but could not make any out. Just then, our hostess appeared from one of the doors. We had not seen or heard her all day and had wondered what had become of her. Smiling but without a word, she motioned for us to follow her. At the end of the long corridor she opened a heavy door on the right side, switched on the light, and asked us to follow her downstairs. There, in the middle of a secluded room we found a table with two benches. She switched on a little radio. The voice announced that a large formation of American planes was heading toward Dresden. We held our breath. " Oh, God!" I thought. "This is the last thing we need right now." The long silence which followed was almost as frightening as the impact of explosions.

Our hostess, sitting across from us with tightly clasped hands and a stern expression, suddenly started to giggle as the broadcaster gleefully announced that our anti-aircraft guns had shot down the lead plane—in those days radar was not yet standard equipment—and the American bombers had dropped their bombs harmlessly on the fields outside town. Soon the all-clear sounded, and we thanked our hostess for having looked after us with such great kindness and care. Mutti asked for her name and address, which she gave us with a smile. "I hope one day I can do something for you to repay your kindness," Mutti told her as she warmly shook the little lady's hand.

She smiled again. "Don't mention it. It was nothing much. I do this sort of thing all the time. Now take good care of your daughters, Frau Zimmermann, and bring them safely to Munich."

"I will," said Mutti.

With suitcases in hand, we followed her up the stairs and to the big front entrance, where we waved our last goodbyes.

51

The Journey to Munich

Mutti could find the train station in the dark, since she had just gone there in the afternoon. When we arrived, the scene she described had not changed. Every platform was packed with people. The train heading south, for which we had tickets, was still there but hopelessly overcrowded. There would be no room for us. With eagle eye Mutti looked around and on the other side of the platform to our left spotted a Red Cross train guarded by two young officers.

Without a moment's hesitation, she walked over to them and showed them first one and then another piece of paper. While the soldiers were looking at the papers, she pulled a pack of cigarettes out of her coat pocket, offered them a smoke, and appeared to ask them for a light. It had turned cold again, which we felt mainly in our toes as we watched Mutti gesticulating with obvious emotion while the officers puffed on their cigarettes and looked at her attentively. As a last resort, Mutti pulled out a half-empty bottle of cognac from her bag and offered the men a drink. Laughing, they each took a swig and handed the bottle back to Mutti. Then we saw them talking with her for a while.

When she came back, her cheeks were flushed red, and she was breathing rapidly. The train, she reported, was reserved for wounded military personnel being evacuated to Army hospitals in Bavaria. The doors on both sides had been sealed and would stay that way until the Red Cross trucks arrived with their cargo.

"Now listen! The two of them came up with a clever solution. After I begged them—told them both our husbands were officers fighting on the Eastern Front, that Gerda was expecting a baby any time, that we had to get out of this overcrowded city where we had no place to stay, and that we had been invited to live with a family outside Munich—they said we would have to take the underpass to the next platform to get to the other side of the train. In the meantime, they would talk with the guard inside the train and get him to open a window. They would then lift the three of us and our baggage in through the window."

We couldn't help laughing. What a solution that was! Still, we had no alternative except to follow their instructions. The guards showed up as promised and were strong enough to heave us, bag and baggage, into the train. Mutti and I were worried about Gerda, but she was the first one through. The men took special care with her and got help from their colleague inside. "Thank God!" Mutti said, laughing and relieved, when we were all inside. Then she added, "Thank you, gentlemen, for helping us in such a creative manner. We shall never forget it." Then she gave them one of her last packs of cigarettes, which they accepted, laughing; we shook hands through the still-open window; and they hurried back to their post.

We sat down and took some deep breaths. We had been rescued again. It did take a while, though, until all the wounded soldiers were brought on board, and the train could move out of the station.

It was past ten, but after all the excitement we were too wound up to fall asleep. So we began talking.

""Wasn't it strange," I led off, "that only we and that lady were all alone in that big building when people all

223

over town were looking for a place to stay?"

"Other tenants may have been out working," Mutti suggested.

"But Mutti, when the air raid started it was almost seven at night. Some of them should have been home by then. Also, we and our hostess were the only ones in the basement."

"Lore is right," Gerda nodded. "I wondered about that too. Our bedroom was nicely furnished with antiques, but we did not see or hear anybody else from the other rooms behind the closed doors."

"Even the kitchen looked unused when I went there to heat water for the tea," Mutti added with a bemused expression. "Well, we won't solve this riddle tonight. The important thing is we got the help we needed in another impossible situation. Don't think about it anymore and just thank God. Our safe arrival in Munich is all we can hope for now. If we survive this war, we'll try to find out more about this woman. She did give me her address."

The dim light and the rattling of the train finally helped us fall asleep. With the first rays of the sun, however, we were once again wide awake. A soldier sitting next to me in the window seat had opened the curtain to look out. He had one arm in a sling. He asked us where we were coming from. When we told him our story, he said we were very lucky. After all, we were the only civilians on the train. We agreed.

Around noon we suddenly stopped somewhere north of Nuremberg. Jumping up, our soldier shouted, "American planes!" He ran to the door, opened it, and yelled for us to come quickly. One by one he pushed us out into the deep snow, then jumped himself. There was no time to think. We simply reacted. In a matter of minutes, perhaps seconds, we heard the impact of machine-gun fire from above on the train. After that, it became very quiet again. Daring to get up, we shook off the wet clumps of snow.

"Those bastards!" Someone yelled. "They have some nerve attacking a Red Cross train!"

As for us, we didn't have the energy to get angry as we tried to climb back into our compartment. We were grateful to be alive and thanked our companion for his quick reaction. Then we noticed all the bullet holes on our side of the compartment. They had hit just where we had been sitting. We trembled at the thought of what might have happened.

Mutti closed her eyes and leaned her head back against the wall. I heard her whispering to herself: "Total War! So this is what Total War is all about. No one follows the Geneva Code anymore."

Our companion overheard Mutti too. "Ja, they do this all the time. After they've dropped their bombs, some of them on the way home dive down and attack trains and even houses with their machine guns. In Wuerzburg recently some women were killed in this way through their open windows as they were cooking dinner."

"Well, the crowds had cheered when Hitler asked if they wanted Total War," Mutti remembered. "But people then did not really know what Total War meant. Now they know!"

After this incident I made a silent pledge to God that I would be confirmed in a Christian Church if we survived the war.

We were hungry, but there were only a few rolls left over from the day before. Since Gerda needed food the most, we gave them to her. Mutti and I each just had a bite and drank some peppermint tea, which was still a little warm.

We made several more stops in the course of the day but were spared further attacks from the air. It was nearly 10 p.m. when we arrived in Munich. As we walked toward the great hall of the station, the air-raid sirens greeted us. An air-raid warden came over to show us the way to the underground shelter. Soon the long bunker was filled with people. Luckily, we had arrived early and were able to find a stretcher for Gerda to lie down on and chairs for us. An old woman offered us a hot drink with milk. With that I fell asleep so deeply that I never heard the detonation of the bombs all around us. We awoke very early the next morning to the stale air in the shelter. After another hot drink, we couldn't get out fast enough.

When we looked around, we saw that the train station was still intact as was Munich's well-known department store, Hertie, across the street. Everything else lay in rubble. As we were looking around for public transportation, an elderly man approached us and said *"Gruess Gott!"* ["May God greet you!"], the Bavarian way to say hello.

"There won't be any busses today," he told us in a thick Bavarian accent. "The bombing last night saw to that."

We told him we wanted to get to Gruenwald.

"Ach, so!" He replied. "Then you have to take this little trolley which we set up this morning. It will take you to a narrow-gauge train station, and from there it will only be 35 minutes to Hoellriegelskreuth. It's on the left bank

of the Isar, just across from Gruenwald. When you get off, you'll have to walk across the stone bridge to the village—that is, if the bridge is still there."

We thanked the man and followed his directions. We felt odd in our little toy train. It took one little wagon merely to carry our baggage. Still, we marveled at how well organized everything was and how it continued to function after last night's air raid.

It only took a half hour until our next "train" arrived to transport us to a place whose name sounded to me like a tongue twister—Hoellriegelskreuth! When we arrived and got off, the air smelled fresh from the new-fallen snow. The sky was now a cloudless blue, and we had only to walk about one hundred meters—a little longer than an American football field—to reach the pine-covered high bank of the Isar River. There to our joy we saw that the stone bridge, an attractive arched structure, was still standing. A steep path with wooden steps led down to it. Mutti went first to make sure there was no slippery ice under the snow cover. Gerda went next so I could keep an eye on her. We stopped for a little while part way to rest and also to look through the opening in the forest which gave a beautiful view of the other side.

There it was, Gruenwald—a place that would be our safe haven for many years to come, my home until I left for America in the fall of 1963. There it was, greeting us after a horrendous but ultimately successful journey, with its church steeple and castle tower embedded in a sparkling landscape of snow-covered pine trees. To me it looked like a late Christmas card come to life. I then realized that we had been protected the whole time and sincerely thanked God for all the people He had put in our path so that we could all see this scene today. Merry Christmas indeed!

52

The First Christmas of Peace*

When I look back on the many blessed, fun-filled Christmases of my childhood and adult life, one will always be the most memorable: Christmas Eve 1945. The first Christmas of Peace.

Our small family—Vati, Mutti, Oma Lina, my sister Gerda, Baby Olaf, and I—had survived the inferno of war. We had fled from the easternmost corner of the Third Reich with only hand luggage and, after harrowing trips, had found refuge in January 1945 in the resort village of Gruenwald, fourteen miles south of the Bavarian capital, Munich.

After months of uncertainty, food shortages, and curfews that followed the unconditional surrender of Germany, life started to become a little more organized and normal. In November 1945, schools reopened their doors, and public transportation was restored amid the rubble of our badly damaged cities. To our great relief and joy, Vati was installed on November 1 by the American Military Government as the principal of the Gruenwald village school.   (Mutti had had the presence of mind to pack the papers from a lawsuit against him for refusing as a school

---

*This chapter was originally published as "The Christmas That Found Peace" in the December 25, 1995 Sunday *Minneapolis Star-Tribune* to honor the 50th anniversary of the first Christmas after World War II.

official to join the Nazi Party.) At last there was a steady family income to look forward to. On December 1, the beginning of Advent that year, we left our small apartment and moved into the spacious principal's quarters in the school building.

There we were with our meager belongings: a few suitcases and flowerpots but no furniture. In those days you could not buy anything like that; you could only "organize," or exchange, goods. Unfortunately, we had nothing to exchange. So we moved in with our five cots, straw mattresses, and a few army blankets. In the living room there was a little iron stove with an exhaust funnel that went out the window. This device had been installed by the caretaker, because the school's heating system had been damaged in an air raid. This little oven had to heat the entire three-bedroom apartment.

Our initial luxuries were an electric oven and an old kitchen table. One day, however, the mayor's office called to inform us that we could purchase German Army surplus furniture very cheaply. Soon better beds, an old sofa, a few bookshelves, and even pictures for the walls were moved in. Above all, there was a big oak desk for Vati. It remained his proud possession until his death in 1964. Finally, a week before Christmas in that year of 1945, the bare living-room windows were decorated with long, russet-colored paper curtains which Gerda had "organized" from somewhere and which looked like real material.

So we were all set for the Christmas celebration. Only good food, Christmas cookies, the tree, and the candles to go with it were missing. But on the last day of school, Vati's students presented him with a four-foot pine tree, some clip-on candleholders complete with white wax candles, and a little bit of tinsel. I shall never forget Vati's face, beaming with joy, as he brought these treasures into the living room. What a wonderful gift! No one had expected any Christmas decorations this year.

My mother had saved all the meat coupons from the week so that on Christmas Eve we might enjoy one hotdog each with potatoes, a little cabbage, and a cup of peppermint tea. The lights were lit, and Vati read the Christmas story from Luke's Gospel as he had done for so many years. Then, with lumps in our throats and wet eyes, we tried to sing all the old Christmas carols. We were grateful for so many things—our lives, being together as a family with our bodies still intact, our new home, Vati's job—things which nowadays people take for granted but which at that time seemed like a miracle to us.

Our hearts were sad, however, as we remembered our lost homeland, East Prussia, and the friends and relatives who had died there under the most terrible circumstances. These civilians were used as scapegoats by the conquering Red Army to pay for the crimes of the Nazis. Very few of the remaining German population were left alive, while the largest share of those who fled ended up in what became Communist East Germany. Moreover, East Prussia itself did not survive but was divided up between Russia, which got the northern part including the harbor city of Koenigsberg (now Kaliningrad) and Poland, which annexed the southern portion, where I was born and grew up. We were truly lucky to be alive.

So, after our family celebration, we decided to go to midnight Mass in the village's little Catholic church overlooking the Isar River valley. This church was only a ten-minute walk from the schoolhouse, while our Lutheran church was out of reach, since the trolleys stopped running at 10 p.m. In honor of the Holiday, the occupation government had lifted the curfew.

I've never seen such a crowded church, before or

since. Waiting to get in, we and many others lined up outside in the bitter 10-degree-Fahrenheit cold. The people who came that night were from all over Germany and even other parts of Europe. Many had been stranded in the Munich area at the end of the War. And never have I witnessed such an eager, sincere, humble group worshiping together in complete surrender and harmony. Even though we represented different countries and denominations—Catholic, Protestant, Orthodox—it didn't seem to matter.

As we entered the big front door, we saw the simple wooden manger with life-size figures of the Holy Family and the Three Kings aglow in warm candlelight. Powerful organ music filled the church along with clouds of incense and the aroma of fresh-cut pine branches. As I looked around, I noticed many women with drawn, lined faces making them look older than they probably were. All were dressed in black, with black hats, veils, or kerchiefs. Tears rolled down their cheeks as their lips moved in silent prayer. The Mass itself was sung by stars from the Munich Opera. To me, a child of fourteen, it seemed as if a choir of angels had descended from heaven that Christmas Eve. And when "Silent Night" echoed through the church, not a single eye remained dry.

Afterward, we walked home through a moonless night under sparkling stars. The snow made crackling sounds beneath our shoes. We especially enjoyed all the flickering candles in the windows, a sight we had missed so much during the long, dark nights of war, when total blackouts were required.

Our hearts filled with hope for a better future and a new beginning. We held on tightly to one another as the wind blew briskly through our torn coats. Yet the Star of Bethlehem had become a new reality for us that Christmas

Eve and seemed to warm our entire being.

A German proverb says, "Except for the night, we could never know the stars." Now we had peace, peace at last!

53

EPILOGUE

1999 – The Homeland Revisited

My daughter Christine and I had planned this trip for over a year. Working for a travel agency in Portland, Oregon, at the time, she could get a free trip for herself plus free Eurail Passes for both of us.

We left from Portland on September 20th, Vati's birthday. Our Lufthansa flights eventually took us to Munich, where we visited my nephew Olaf and picked up Liesbeth, Marga's sister, who would be our interpreter. Educated in a Polish high school in Osterode, she had left in the late Fifties and settled in Munich. Consequently, she was fluent in Polish as well as German. We paid her roundtrip train fare in exchange for her services, which included making arrangements with Polish friends to put us up in their house on the Uckelsee (Lake Uckel).

After a two-day stay in the Bavarian capital, we took the night train—a 1st-class sleeper-coach—to Berlin, where we transferred the next morning to a Polish train. In Posen we changed trains again, this time for our final destination, Olsztyn—the Allenstein of my youth. Posen had the gloomy look of a city still recovering from war. Soon we were on our way to Thorun, and from there it did not take long to get to where we were going.

It was a sunny afternoon. Suddenly I noticed the beginning of Lake Drawence. And from here the experience of my return truly began. It is hard to describe the feeling of returning to the place of one's youth 54 years later. It's more dream than reality.

Before we knew it, the train rolled into the Olsztyn Station. On disembarking, we were greeted by a tall young man, who kissed our hands, took my suitcase, and motioned for us to follow him down the stairs. I glanced at the platform. These were the very stones we walked on so long ago as had Oma and Opa before us. I felt a little shaky. As we walked through the big hall and out into the sunlight, I could see that everything looked different. There were new buildings across the street where a big hotel had once stood, and one side of the station was also rebuilt.

Soon we were standing beside a big, modern station wagon, where the young man loaded our baggage. Rushing to keep up, I stumbled and landed, though not too hard, on my knees. Tante Hanna, I remembered suddenly, had never made it out of this station. In an attempt to get up, I felt as though my hands were stuck to the ground. There was a lump in my throat as I spontaneously whispered, "Forgive us our sins as we forgive those who sin against us."

"Mutti, what are you doing?" I heard Christine's voice and quickly got up. Suddenly I felt as if a load had been lifted from my back. I got into the car. The young man—son of our host family, as Liesbeth explained—sped through town. As I watched, familiar landmarks flew by. The hilly street down to Lake Uckel was still there, lined as in my day with old houses. In front of one, which I had always noticed when I took the streetcar to the Lake, stood the same statue of the Madonna. It had somehow survived the ravages of war. Amazing!

Once at "our" house, we were greeted by our hostess, Jadwiga Kowalczyk, and her daughter-in-law, a pretty brunette with large blue eyes. Jadwiga first embraced her old friend Liesbeth, then led us to the living room, where a long table loaded with huge quantities of food awaited the hungry travelers. (The Poles had always been known for their generous hospitality in Europe.) We were not really that hungry after having sat all day in the trains, but our appetites perked up after the first delicious bites. Before long, Liesbeth was busy translating as we pulled out our gifts for the family members. Then we were shown to our rooms upstairs. Jadwiga had given us the master bedroom. What an honor! Here we would sleep under soft, white goose-down comforters. Her husband worked as a night watchman at the nearby college, where he had a bed he could use. Liesbeth meanwhile was given a small bedroom down the hall from us.

It was still early, but we had had a long day and were exhausted. Christine fell asleep right away. I lay there unable to. My mind raced. We were actually here. Unbelievable! The full moon shining through the large window with the billowing see-through curtain helped keep me wide awake. I got up and looked out. Below was Jadwiga's garden with the last flowers of summer caught in the silver light. Behind them, a meadow stretched to a pine grove with scattered birch trees standing white and tall. It was magical.

The young man had told us that the weather forecast was not very good. The sky was still clear, and I prayed hard that it would stay that way. After all, we had only three-and-a-half days to be here. So, when I went down to breakfast the next morning, I was pleased to see sunlight streaming through the window. I hoped it would last.

Jadwiga, who had taken the day off from her part-time job at the House of Culture, showed us the way to the bus stop at the bottom of the hill. She had also been thoughtful enough to buy us a book of bus coupons. Before we knew it, we were in the center of town. As it happened, the bus stopped right in front of the Treudank Theater, the place I had wanted to see the most. Although the front was now covered with wild grape leaves, I still recognized this important oasis of my childhood. Hurrying up the stone steps, I saw the colorful posters announcing future plays.

When we reached the top, we found the doors locked. As we were about to turn and leave, a door opened. A young man with a dachshund on a leash approached us. He asked us something in Polish, probably what we wanted. Liesbeth quickly told him my childhood history with the theater and said we wanted to buy four tickets for the show the day after tomorrow, which he soon brought us. The fourth ticket would be for Jadwiga's daughter, whom we invited and who drove us. The play was of course in Polish. I didn't care. I just wanted to be inside for old time's sake.

Next I wanted to see Oma Lina's house. To get there, we had to walk through an underpass beneath the railroad tracks. It was the same one Oma Lina and I would use years ago to go to the farmers' market, only now it was worn and dirty. After walking up a hilly street, we found Oma's apartment building. It was still standing but showed lots of battering from the War. I looked up to Oma's third-floor window. There she would always sit in the afternoon, doing her needle work.

I had so many memories connected with this town. As I walked around and saw more familiar places, it was as if Mutti, Vati, and their parents were walking along with me, whispering stories from their youth in my ear. They themselves had never had the opportunity to revisit the old homeland, since the borders to Poland were closed to Germans for many years after the war.

The whole block of the former Hohenzollern-damm, where Oma Dorchen's apartment building had once stood, had been leveled by air mines. The iron railroad bridge had been bombed out too. In its place there was now a plain stone bridge. The vision I had had on Oma's roof back in 1943 had come true.

I took some pictures. Then we went down the Bahnhofstrasse to the former Kaiser-Wilhelm-Allee. This was the very walk I took every morning to get to Frau Professor Mann's for my year of illegal private instruction. It now seemed much shorter than I remembered, but of course now I wasn't worried about running into my old classmates. Amazing! The building was still there. As I was taking a picture from across the street, a man stopped near us and said something to me in Polish. Liesbeth laughed. "He wants to know why you are taking a picture of an old building when you could be taking one of him. He needs a new wife, he says." He grinned, and I waved him off. In a way, though, it was a compliment, since I had looked to him like a native of the town and not a foreigner.

As we proceeded, I soon saw Vati's old high school on the left—a pretty redbrick building with high Gothic windows. We sat down on a bench in front of it under shady chestnut trees. "My feet hurt from all the walking," Liesbeth complained. I turned to Christine: "Look at all the public buildings like this school, the police station, and the post office—even the churches. They were all built with your great grandfather's bricks—that was his business—and they survived two world wars."

We next walked through the high medieval gate

into the old part of the city. The market square I found had been converted into a large outdoor café, with tables and chairs scattered around. As we walked toward an empty table, an elderly woman stopped us. "I overheard you speaking German," she said in our mother tongue and handed us a little two-page German newsletter. "Why don't you come to Gruenwald [the former Hohenstein] next week? German and Polish citizens will be getting together to sing the old folksongs."

We were surprised and laughed. "We'd like to," I replied, "but we have to leave in two days. Do you live here?"

She nodded. "I was born here and made it through the end of the War. Of course, it was not easy." Wishing her well, we took our leave and headed to a table in the shade, where we had tea and wrote postcards home. Meanwhile, the people around us were enjoying the mild autumn sun.

Behind Market Square, to the right, I could make out the little Gothic Evangelical Lutheran Church where Vati had been baptized, he and Mutti confirmed, and Gerda married (in 1944). It was astounding that none of the churches had been damaged by the War. I was eager to go inside. Once in, I was surprised by how small it was. It had seemed much larger in my memory. There was not much of the old church to see, since the interior had been totally restored. The street in front led to the entrance of the Castle, which unfortunately was closed for the day. We would have to leave that visit for tomorrow.

A sumptuous meal with assorted meats and all kinds of salads awaited us. After, we showed each other family pictures and, with Liesbeth's help, made conversation. When the young couple shared their wedding album, I was able to respond with the little book I had put together from photos of Marianna's wedding in Hawaii. The main difference was that the Polish ceremony had taken place in front of a justice of the peace, with the bride wearing a long red silk gown, while Marianna had been dressed in white in front of a Christian minister with the Pacific Ocean behind them. (The red dress made it clear that the family belonged to the Communist Party. We did not care. They were kind people who were very generous in their hospitality to us.) At the end of the evening, Jadwiga gave us a coffee-table book with photos of and multi-lingual explanations about Olsztyn.

The weather behaved itself. So the next day we returned to the city castle, which I had last seen when I was nine. When I saw it, I remembered the big statue in the entrance hall of Nikolas Copernicus, the famous medieval astronomer. In our day, Germany claimed him as a German. Now the Poles were claiming him for Poland. He was probably a mixture like me and most of my fellow East Prussians.

After touring the castle, we walked around the area, this time doing some shopping in a store specializing in amber, for which the Baltic, including the former East Prussia, was famous. Again, we ended up in a café, across from the old newspaper building where Mutti had once worked. In the background was the magnificent castle surrounded by old-growth trees. Over coffee and cake, we watched the people passing by. Across the street were mainly girls in blue jeans, many with blond ponytails. They carried their school books in briefcases and backpacks.

"Look, Christine," I said. "That's how your grandma once walked to her school just around the corner." As I took the whole scene in, the façade of the houses unchanged from my childhood, Shakespeare's famous line from *As You Like It* went through my head:

"All the world's a stage,/ And all the men and women merely players." Yes, it was the same scene and the same action; only the players had changed.

The next morning we breakfasted early so that Jadwiga's son could drive us to Kajkowo (Kiefernberg) to visit my old school friend Marga. Our excursion took us through hilly country with alternating woods and meadows. We made a stop by Lake Drawence in Ostroda (the former Osterode). There, in a new-looking restaurant, the father and son could take their morning beer. I pointed to the place where Mutti's birth house had stood. We also made a quick visit to the local museum, which had photos of the town from the early years of the 20th Century. The view had not changed much. It was here that both my maternal and paternal grandparents had met. We found a bench overlooking the lake and sat down. The mild autumn sun caused the water to look like a silver mirror. Ducks and majestic swans glided by. We took some photos.

We began walking towards Marga's house. I remembered it as a long walk, but now it seemed short. The old landmarks were still there. The Jewish cemetery with the iron gate seemed unharmed from the War. Next, on the right, came the garrison, which also looked the same, with young officers smartly walking through the yard. Only the uniforms had changed.

Soon we reached the edge of town. Below was our old village, with the school in the foreground. The building looked bare to me with the big trees which had surrounded it gone. Liesbeth said the white letters on the front said it was now an agricultural institute. I had to laugh, since the formerly cultivated fields all around were overgrown with weeds. By this time we were standing in front. Looking at the windows of what had been our apartment on the second floor, I had an insuperable urge to go inside. The entrance stood open, so I approached a group of students. One spoke English. She called over a teacher who spoke German. I asked permission to see the rooms upstairs. She explained that they were classrooms now and were being used. She did however lead me to one that happened to be empty. It was our former dining room, at one end of which our master bedroom had stood. I quickly took a picture out the front window.

Vati's former *Herrenzimmer* was now part of the corridor. The big window was still there, though. Suddenly memories flooded over me, and I felt shaky. The big staircase was gone, and the interior had been completely changed. I had to get out of there. Hastily thanking the teacher for her kindness, I went back outside.

We now walked the familiar street to the center of the village. Everything looked the same except that the old war monument had been replaced by a statue of the Virgin Mary—a great change so far as I was concerned. Some houses were gone, like the big grocery store that had belonged to the mayor. Walking slowly down the street that led to the lake, I noticed that my friend Annemie's red-brick house had since been painted white. Looking to the right, I saw that the building which belonged to Margot's family had been leveled to the ground. Maybe there had been some fighting here at the end of the War.

Soon we found ourselves in front of Marga's house, which itself fronted the lake. My heart leapt for joy. Her son had built her a retirement cottage next to the old homestead. It was surrounded by a garden filled with vegetables and beautiful flowers. Giving us a big hug, Marga gasped. "I can't believe it. You are finally here, Lorchen!" She had tears in her eyes. I placed a lei of silk flowers around her neck, kissed her, and said "Aloha!" as I gave her a bottle of cologne. I also handed her a small bottle of German champagne and her husband, Josef, a bottle of Jaegermeister schnapps, which he seemed to appreciate very much.

Since it was lunchtime, she served us home-made chicken soup, with both the chicken and the vegetables from her garden. Streuselkuchen and coffee followed. Talking about old times, we seemed to be teenagers again. After, one of here grandsons, who could speak English, walked us down to the lakeshore. "It has shrunk quite a bit from our time, Lorchen," Liesbeth explained, "because the village has used the water for irrigation and other purposes." I could see that. We took several pictures and returned to Marga's cottage. Her round face reminded me of the ancient stone sculpture of a native woman I had seen the day before in the castle courtyard. Despite famines and wars, Marga was still here—the people were still here— tending to the land of their ancestors.

It was three o'clock, and our car was waiting. Time to leave if we were to make the play that evening. We were a bit disappointed that the performance took place in a small secondary theater and not the main hall. Fortunately, an English-speaking employee permitted me to go into the big theater, where a rehearsal was in progress, and look down from the balcony at the stage where I had danced as a child. Of course, 60 years had wrought changes. Instead of red plush, the seats were now covered with a cheap plastic material, and the carpets were a dull beige.

Back in the little theater, we took our first-row seats for a play by a contemporary Danish playwright. The words had been translated into Polish. During the intermission, Liesbeth gave us a summary of the plot. I enjoyed watching the performance and listening to the sound of the language as spoken by trained actors. Of course, at close range as we were, we sometimes felt as well as heard the results of their professional articulation.

The next morning was another early call for breakfast. We took our final photos in front of the house, and then it was off to the train station for the trip back to Munich. Our host family was delighted with our donation of Deutsch Marks—this was just before the introduction of the Euro—which was worth twice as much in Polish currency. Just before our train pulled out, the daughter-in-law showed up to wish us goodbye. There were big hugs all around. They were all just wonderful people.

The trained picked up speed as it headed north out of the city. This time we passed Osterode (Ostroda) and Lake Drawence, which was unchanged and looked as beautiful as 60 years before with its surrounding forest. Somehow nature remains unchanged as do the flight patterns of migratory birds, which neither know nor respect the borders set and re-set by us human beings.

Before long we left the Oberland with its hilly meadows and fields and entered the Weichsel River plain, with the old Crusader castles to the East. I pointed them out to Christine, but with the train now moving quickly, they disappeared before she could see them. She took a deep breath. The whole experience had been something new for her—a trip into a different world. Up till now she had known only the southern and western parts of historic Germany.

We rolled comfortably across long bridges over first the Weichsel, then the Oder Rivers. I remembered how Vati, Uncle Erich, and Oma Dorchen had crossed these same bridges in an old, unheated military train in the freezing cold of January 1945.

Hungry for lunch, we made our way to the dining car. I pointed to items on the English and German menus but let Liesbeth order in Polish. I didn't want to speak German, since at the table behind us was a group of Polish soldiers already high on beer. One never knew how they might react! When the young chef personally delivered my plate, replete with slices of orange and watermelon, I said in English, "Oh, California style!" For some reason he answered, "No German ever lived in the country we have just left." I gave him an ambiguous smile. As we walked back to our compartment, Liesbeth commented, "The Poles have tried to wipe out any trace of German culture. They have even leveled the Germany cemeteries. My grandmother's gravestone in Kiefernberg is not there anymore. I had to memorize the spot."

"Well," I replied. "They can't wipe out our German architecture. This young man can't be blamed. He was born years after the War. All he knows is what he was taught in school."

I leaned back on my seat. The food in my stomach coupled with the rattling of the train made me drowsy. Memories went through my head about our family vacations on the Baltic Sea, especially the last one on the Kurische Nehrung. It was part of Russia now and, as I had heard, was home to a large defense installation. The bird sanctuary was probably long gone. Agnes Migel's poem, "The Women of Nidden," came to mind. I wondered about the fate of the simple people there at War's end. My question took the form of a poem.

> *Who witnessed your agony,*
> *Young women and girls of Nidden?*
> *Who heard your desperate cries*
> *When you became the prey of vengeful cruelty?*
> *Were the dunes refuge enough*
> *Like those in ancient times?*
> *Or did you flee with your pain and sorrow*

Into the welcoming arms of Mother Sea?
Few will know beyond the elks guarding the shore.

As from a distance I heard Liesbeth talking with a fellow passenger in Polish. Christine was listening to a music tape. I drifted off again. This time memories from early childhood arose—from the first village I lived in. They seemed like a fairytale.

The Village

A long time ago, when I was a little girl, I lived in a small village. It lay in the midst of farmland, meadows, and swamps. Round about were thick forests and many lakes with crystal-clear water. Located in the southernmost part of the German province of East Prussia, the village was close to the Polish border. A cool brook ran through the village and irrigated the fields until entering the nearby lake. This brook gave the village its name, "Kaltenborn," or "cold brook." Since many local residents spoke Polish as well as German, the village had a second name, "Zimna Woda," which meant the same thing in Polish. These inhabitants generally had Polish surnames, since their forefathers, like many other European Protestants in Catholic areas, had been forced to leave their homeland in order to settle in East Prussia, with its official policy of religious tolerance.

All the important buildings in this hamlet had been built of red brick. Examples included the State Forestry Office and the public school. The latter had once been a large farmhouse that was abandoned after World War I.

As a result, the school grounds included two large barns, used mainly by storks who would visit in the spring as they worked their way back north. Another brick building was the saw mill with its attached lumberyard, where many of the village's men worked. Large brick farmhouses also lined the main street.* In the midst of them were two inns, also of brick. One contained the local grocery store, where one could buy small gift items and knick-knacks as well as food. The same inn had an attached ballroom. Last but not least came the brick house and office of the village's guardian of law and order, Officer Fritz Leidereither. The older people called him our gendarme, a term left over from the French occupation following World War I. Since there wasn't much police work for him to do, he spent most of his time as a successful beekeeper.

Another brick building in the center of the village, across from the wooden bell tower, housed the butcher. There, clad in his blood-spotted long, white coat, he would provide meat for the tables of the villagers. Next door lived Miss Luise, the Evangelical Lutheran deaconess, who served as the village nurse. She looked after the physical well being of her little community with bandages, plasters, castor oil, enemas, and the like. She would also treat common colds or flus with herb teas, cold leg wraps, and other common country remedies. This slender woman in her ankle-length blue dress could be seen striding through the village each day, though never without her bonnet of starched white organza. The hat, tied with white bands in a fluffy bowknot under her chin, made her seem taller than she was and also served to soften her handsome but stern features. Catholics called these Lutheran community nurses "Protestant nuns."

---

*Unlike American farms, where the farmhouses are adjacent to the fields, German farmers have their houses in town, preferring to travel back and forth each day to their fields.

The big bell in the wooden tower would ring out dark, deep-throated tones for a villager being carried to his final resting place or short, happy ones when a baby was born. This bell was the only remnant of the old church, burnt down with most of the farmhouses by the Cossacks during World War I. One of the few structures to survive was the present school. Thus the place had become a village without church or pastor. For special occasions, to be sure, a minister was borrowed from one of the nearby towns. Deaconess Luise functioned as instructor for the confirmation classes. By the time my father became village schoolmaster in 1933, the village had risen from the ashes and was bustling once again.

This was the place where my first impressions of life were formed, the microcosm of my childhood. When I read fairy tales, they all took place in the enchanted forests surrounding this village. My lively imagination produced bewitched castles, haunted houses, and magicians galore that filled the woods of Kaltenborn.

Today this village lives only in my memory. What World War I was unable to do, World War II completed. Nature has reclaimed this place on the border between Eastern and Western Europe like so many other battlefields over the thousands of years of history. Mother Earth has gently spread a blanket of moss and flowers across this place which had once hosted a human community. Only here and there fragments of a cross now appeared.

The wind in the woods united with sweet birdsong will provide an everlasting lullaby for all the fallen heroes of the various fatherlands who rest in this place—young men at the beginning of their adult lives, robbed of the chance to realize their own visions and dreams by power-hungry leaders and politicians and their false promises of glory.

But who knows? Maybe this village for the dead will once more become a village of the living in the endless cycle of life and death, endings and beginnings. Only time will tell.

I opened my eyes and looked out the window of the onrushing train. Yes, this was a land in the middle, where wars of conquest and re-conquest had swept back and forth for hundreds of years. People here had come to accept them as natural occurrences, like severe thunderstorms or forest fires. How wise of the new German Government, I thought, to give up all claims to this land in perpetuity despite the pain the loss had given to the remaining German farmers, the descendants of those who had worked this beloved soil for over 800 years.

Most people will never understand that forgiveness has more power than revenge, which simply causes an endless cycle of revenge and counter-revenge. Will humankind ever learn?

> *What do we want?*
> *What do we need the most?*
> *It is peace, peace for the whole world.*
> *It is not the violence of the storm*
> *But the gentleness of the morning dew*
> *That makes for a clear day.*
> *Don't shout "peace" loudly in the streets.*
> *Let peace whisper in your hearts.*
> *Let peace conquer your hearts!*
> *Thus peace like the morning dew*
> *Will cover the crust of the Earth.*

(Written in Holden Village, Washington – summer 1993)

Acknowledgments

When you drink water, remember the mountain spring.
(Chinese proverb)

There are many people to thank for helping this little book become a reality. First come all my relatives and friends who populate its pages as well as my memories. Without them I would have had nothing to write about. I must again give special acknowledgment to my parents, who made it possible for me to survive the Hitler years and the War with my body, mind, and soul intact. Many were not so lucky. Then, I must thank my children—Marianna, Christine, and Harper—and my granddaughter, Sarah, who recently turned five. I originally wrote this book for them. But as I began reading chapters to friends, they suggested I make it available for a wider readership, including themselves. So, thanks to all of you, I have now followed this suggestion.

When it became clear that life would not grant me the time to edit all the chapters, members of the nonprofit Wisdom Factors International encouraged me to put together an "Excerpts" version representing about 50% of the book, which they would then publish for family and friends. I was pleased that in this way I would likely have the chance to hold a copy in my hand before leaving. In this regard, special thanks are due to Mr. M. Jan Rumi, president of Wisdom Factors International, for his unstinting support and to the Most Reverend Stephen Randolph Sykes, Bishop of the Inclusive Orthodox Church, who, between daily church and monastic business, was able to do the graphic design and oversee the production of this initial version of the memoir.

Next, I would like to thank my husband, Dr. Reynold Feldman, who, along with our children, always encouraged me to put my stories down in writing. Not only that, but if my words don't seem to have too much of a German accent, it may stem from the fact that Reynold, with his three degrees in English from Yale, was the editor.

Finally, as I am about to leave this world for the next, I want to make sure to express my thanks to Almighty God, Who, despite its ups and downs, enabled me to see that mine was indeed a wonderful life. If my stories help even one person to understand that all life, regardless of how bad it may seem at any given moment, is a blessing, then my work will not have been in vain.

May the voices of your past lead you to hear the voice of God in your life.

Simone Feldman
Manoa Valley, O'ahu, Hawai'i
August 2006